Can I Grow
POTATOES
IN POTS?

RHS Can I Grow Potatoes in Pots?
Author: Sally Nex
First published in Great Britain in 2022 by Mitchell Beazley, an imprint of
Octopus Publishing Group Ltd, Carmelite House, 50 Victoria Embankment,
London EC4Y 0DZ
www.octopusbooks.co.uk

An Hachette UK Company
www.hachette.co.uk

Published in association with the Royal Horticultural Society
Copyright © 2022 Quarto Publishing plc

ISBN: 978-1-78472-845-8
A CIP record of this book is available from the British Library
Set in Archer and Open Sans
Printed and bound in China

Mitchell Beazley Publisher: Alison Starling
Editorial Assistant: Jeannie Stanley
RHS Publisher: Rae Spencer-Jones
RHS Consultant Editor: Simon Maughan
RHS Head of Editorial: Tom Howard

Conceived, designed and produced by
The Bright Press, Part of the Quarto Group
The Old Brewery, 6 Blundell Street, London, N7 9BH, England
www.Quarto.com

Project Editor: Ruth Patrick
Design and Picture Research: Lindsey Johns

The Royal Horticultural Society is the UK's leading gardening charity
dedicated to advancing horticulture and promoting good gardening.
Its charitable work includes providing expert advice and information,
training the next generation of gardeners, creating hands-on opportunities
for children to grow plants and conducting research into plants, pests
and environmental issues affecting gardeners.

For more information visit www.rhs.org.uk or call 0845 130 4646.

RHS

Can I Grow
POTATOES
IN POTS?

A GARDENER'S COLLECTION
of Handy Hints *to*
Grow Your Own Food

SALLY NEX

MITCHELL BEAZLEY

Contents

1 What to Grow

2 Where to Grow

3 Incredible Edibles

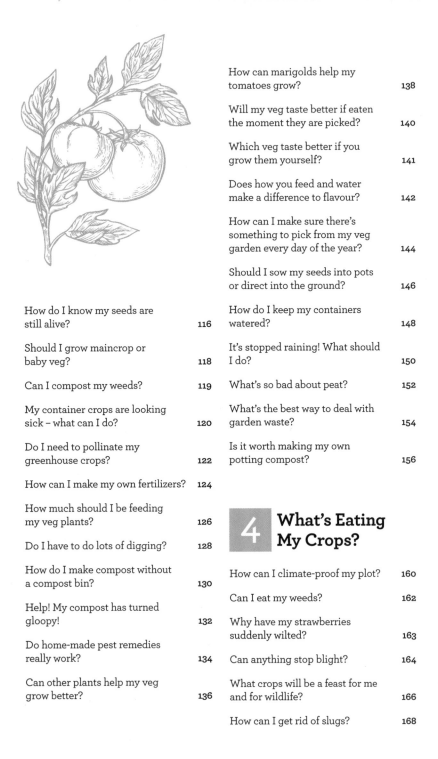

4 What's Eating My Crops?

5 Harvest and Beyond

Introduction

GROWING VEG AIN'T WHAT IT USED TO BE. **A quiet revolution is under way in our veg patches and it's turning the old, comfy world of flat caps, double-digging and ramrod-straight rows on its head.**

Nowadays, flowers, herbs and edible perennials are creeping in among the allotment carrots and cabbages. Traditional monoculture planting is giving way to riotous cottage-garden jumbles where kale and sprouts share a bed with nasturtiums, lettuces and French beans.

You might see a keyhole garden in one corner, or a bed neatly divided into squares, each densely planted with salads. Some veg patches aren't even in the ground: these days you're as likely to find veg growing in windowboxes, on balconies and even on windowsills indoors as edible houseplants. Veg climb up walls, or scramble over the roof, and potatoes grow in pots.

Putting away the spade

We know more about the importance of soil ecosystems and how our plants plug into complex relationships between countless teeming life forms beneath our feet

▼ 21st-century veg growing is all about colour, flavour and variety.

A

QUICK ANSWERS

The 'A' box under each question offers you the quick and dirty answer in the shortest form possible. Read on for the main text, which offers additional context and plenty of extra detail.

Gardening with a lighter touch

Throughout this book, you'll learn how to grow vegetables with a lighter footprint on the earth: how to garden without plastic, in ways that encourage biodiversity and help your veg patch lock away carbon, so making your own contribution to tackling climate change.

You'll also find out how to become more self-reliant, using the resources around you to create compost, save seed and even make garden sundries from beanpoles and trellis to string, plant labels and pots. And you'll discover how the natural world itself can help you protect your plants from pests and boost plant growth to deliver plentiful harvests full of flavour and excitement.

to access nutrients and moisture – so spades are for mulching, not digging, and composting is big. And while growing veg that's showbench perfect is nice, it seems less important these days than flavour, and how good it is for you to eat. So nobody minds a few holes here and there: and some creepy-crawlies are positively welcome.

This new, more relaxed approach to vegetable growing goes hand in hand with modern-day worries about climate change, biodiversity loss and food security. These weren't concerns that troubled Victorian gardeners in the 19th century, with their nicotine-and-sulphur scorched earth approach to gardening, but we've now realized it's not an either/or. You can grow your own food in a way that's positively good for the wider environment.

▶ Grow your own and your food comes just as nature intended: no chemicals, no plastic, no compromise.

Cutting edge gardening

Chapter one is all about gardening at the cutting edge. Your five a day gets so much more exciting when you can grow your own: if you've ever fancied having a go at growing heritage tomatoes, edible flowers, botanicals for boozy cocktails, olives or lemons – this is where you'll find out how.

You'll also find 21st-century veg growing techniques explained, from forest gardening and permaculture to no-dig and lasagne beds, allowing you to garden in harmony with the wider world around you. You'll discover how to harness the power of herbal teas to boost your wellbeing; if you prefer builder's tea, you'll discover how to grow that at home, too.

When you grow in unconventional spaces you need to think sideways, and upwards – so chapter two sends you up the wall and onto the roof to extend your growing space wherever you live. Find out how to co-opt patios, windowsills, fences and hedges for growing food, and explore the amazing range of food you can grow in containers, from fruit trees to potatoes. This is also where you'll find out about innovations like artificial lighting, hydroponics and naturally dwarfing 'patio' varieties, so you can grow food even if you have no garden at all.

▲ Higher temperatures due to climate change are making it more feasible to grow lemons and olives, even in previously cool-climate gardens.

Building self-reliance

Turn to chapter three to find out how to make the most of the resources around you to grow incredible edibles, from creating your own plant fertilizers to techniques that help ensure pollination. Learn those little gardeners' tricks to give you better results for less effort, and read how you can manage your garden to enlist the full power of nature on your side. Partner plants that help each other grow better, turn your soil into a powerhouse rich in natural nutrients and use the magic of recycling to boost every plant in your garden using only materials you probably already have.

In chapter four, you'll learn how nature can also be an invaluable ally against pests and diseases. Read about how to diagnose many of the more common diseases you'll encounter, and what to do about it; and find out how to strike a balance between a healthy garden ecosystem, where slugs and aphids are a valuable part of the food chain, while also guarding your crops so you still have a harvest to pick. Garden alongside and in harmony with your local wildlife and you find natural predators do much of your pest control for you, leaving you free to enjoy planting and harvesting instead.

▼ Growing your own is good for you: the amount of fruit and veg people eat increases by an average of 40 per cent when it's home grown.

Garden yourself green

Finally, in chapter five you can read how to make the most of your harvest. Just by growing your own food you're slashing your carbon footprint, lifting yourself out of the carbon-hungry, high-pollution dependency on intensive agriculture, imports and plastic packaging. Follow the advice in these pages and you'll measure your food miles in metres and eat organic for a fraction of the cost of buying it in the shops. Home-grown food often tastes better, and when it's picked it's at the point of ripeness and cooked within minutes of harvest the nutrients are at their peak, too.

So turn the page to leave Victorian veg growing behind and step into a brave new, gentler and kinder world.

What to Grow

I've never grown vegetables before – where do I start?

SO YOU WANT TO START GROWING YOUR OWN? You're in good company! Millions of new gardeners venture out each year, seed packets in hand, to try growing their own food for the first time. But starting a new veg patch from scratch can be daunting – so where's the best place to begin?

Choose a sunny spot for your first veg bed, clear away any weeds and then add goodness to the soil. Covering the bed with 5–8cm (2–3in) of garden compost or soil improver will give veg seedlings the goodness they need. Don't bother to dig it in; the worms will do that for you.

Start planting from mid-spring. You'll want to grow everything, but choose three or four reliable favourites. Concentrate on growing the veg you most like to eat, learn to grow those well, then get more adventurous.

▼ Sow courgettes in pots on a windowsill indoors, then plant them outside once they're sturdy youngsters and raring to get growing.

FIVE OF THE BEST STARTER VEG

Baby-leaf salads Great in containers and crops within a month.

French beans Heavy-cropping and delicious.

Courgettes Satisfyingly big and ridiculously productive.

Kale The easiest member of the cabbage family to grow.

Chard Just like spinach, but super easy.

The most important thing is not to get too carried away. When you're bursting with enthusiasm, it's easy to take on more than you can cope with: much better to start small, with one or two veg beds or a few containers while you learn the ropes.

Seeds or plug plants?

There are lots of veg that are easy to grow direct from seed: potatoes, beetroot, chard and carrots, for example. Seedlings are particularly vulnerable to slug attacks and drying out, so have a go with seed – but buy a few ready-grown plug (baby) plants from a peat-free supplier as well. Then you know that even if things go wrong while you're learning how to keep seedlings safe, you'll still have a crop to pick. Keep your veg garden watered in dry spells and check regularly for slugs. An insect-proof mesh protects pest-prone brassicas (broccoli, kale and the like), which might save you some heartache.

Picking and (best of all) eating fresh food you've raised yourself is an absolute joy – and you'll soon be wondering what to try next.

▶ Although you'll want to grow absolutely everything, concentrate on a few easy veg while you're still learning the ropes.

TOP TIPS FOR BEGINNER GROWERS

Water seed drills before you sow so your seeds are in damp soil from the start.

Sow into pots and seedtrays to make it more difficult for slugs to find seedlings.

Don't be in a hurry to sow because if you wait until mid-spring, it'll be warmer and seedlings will grow faster.

Have patience if you're starting a new veg patch – it'll take a few seasons for all the goodness you add as mulches each year to build up.

Try not to worry if things don't go as well as you hoped; there's always next year!

How do I choose which tomato to grow?

ONE OF THE DELIGHTS of growing your own is discovering a world of varieties you never knew existed, from purple carrots and spherical cucumbers to stripey tomatoes. But with over 10,000 different tomatoes to choose from, how do you know which to grow?

Each variety of vegetable behaves differently, so it's really important to know what you're growing. Variety governs flavour, but also the way the plants grow, when they produce a crop and how prone they are to disease.

Do your homework

Look out for local tomato festivals or explore greengrocers, farmers' markets and specialist growers where you'll often find named varieties on sale, which you can buy to try.

HOW TO CHOOSE A GOOD VARIETY

Look for AGM on the seed packet This is the Royal Horticultural Society's Award of Garden Merit and means the variety has been extensively trialled before experts gave it the thumbs up.

Do your research Search catalogues or read trusted reviews online to find varieties with qualities you want, perhaps disease resistance, good flavour or a compact habit for growing in containers.

Ask around If you know any experienced veg growers, they'll be delighted to share their must-grow veg varieties with you – and there's no better recommendation than first-hand, local experience!

Once you have a list of a few favourite varieties, look them up in seed catalogues to find out how they grow. If you're growing in containers, bush varieties (known as determinate) are ideal, as they are compact and bushy and don't need extra support. But they almost always produce small cherry tomatoes. For larger tomatoes, you'll need a cordon (indeterminate) variety. These are tall plants that require sturdy supports and regular training – but you'll get heavier crops and a greater range of sizes, colours and flavours.

Major on tried-and-tested tomato varieties. Then add an unusual wild card variety, just for fun: it's fine if it doesn't work out, as you'll still get a harvest from your reliable croppers and there's always another one to try next year!

TOMATOES TO TRY

'Shirley' Go-to salad tom that is super reliable and has an excellent flavour.

'Marmande' Superb French heritage beefsteak with a mouth-watering flavour.

'Sungold' One for the sweet-toothed with cascades of yellow cherry toms.

'Losetto' Bush tomato with outstanding blight resistance and a long harvest.

'Rio Grande' Big, meaty plum tomatoes ideal for cooking.

Blight-resistant varieties prevent you losing your harvest to disease (see page 165), which is especially helpful if you are growing tomatoes outside in a damp climate. In cooler parts of the world, early-maturing varieties like 'Latah', 'Bloody Butcher' or 'Incas' also help boost your chances of picking ripe fruit even in so-so summers. Keep notes and fine-tune your selection each year until you've found the combination that works for you.

I'd love to make my own jam – where do I start?

TUCKING INTO YOUR OWN SWEET, fruity, home-made jam at breakfast is one of the real pleasures of a home-grown lifestyle. So what do you need to grow your own jam and how do you do it?

IT'S ALL ABOUT THE PECTIN

Pectin is a natural substance that keeps fruit cell walls elastic. Once cooked with sugar it turns gelatinous, helping the jam set. So fruits that have naturally high pectin levels – including apples, blueberries, blackberries and loganberries – are easiest to turn into jam. Fruit picked slightly underripe is also higher in pectin.

To make jam from fruit with low pectin levels – such as strawberries, cherries, rhubarb and raspberries – combine with a high-pectin fruit in a two-fruit jam or use jam sugar, which contains added pectin.

Most fruit is perennial, so you plant once and harvest for years. Choose traditional raspberries, strawberries and blackcurrants, or luxury fruits like blueberries, figs, cherries and Japanese wineberries – all pickable from your back garden, delicious fresh and great for jam too.

You won't have to find room for many plants: one loganberry, for example, produces about 8kg (16lb) of fruit a year, while raspberries give you 2.5kg (6lb) per cane (depending on the variety). Strawberries are less productive, but you'll still pick 300–400g (10–14oz) of fruit per plant.

Bramble,
Rubus fruticosus

First, plant some fruit bushes! Most jams are made from soft fruit – among the easiest and most generous plants you can grow. Loganberries, autumn-fruiting raspberries, redcurrants and blackcurrants are particularly heavy croppers and should give you plenty to eat fresh with lots left over for making jam.

Fruit-growing tips

Fruit can either be grouped together in a berry patch or blended into the garden: crab apples make pretty ornamental trees and blackcurrants are handsome shrubs. Grow wineberries against a fence and fill containers with strawberries. Blueberries, which like acidic soil, can be grown in pots of peat-free ericaceous (acidic) compost if your soil is neutral or alkaline: keep damp and grow two varieties for the best crops.

Fruit doesn't require much fuss: mulch in spring and prune once a year (stone fruit – like cherries and plums – in summer; berry fruit – like apples and pears – in winter). Protect from birds, who adore berries as much as you: build a fruit cage or make individual cages for each plant. Just remove once fruiting is over so the birds can take care of pests for you.

FRUIT JAM RECIPE

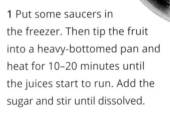

You will need
- 1.5kg (3lb) fruit (unwashed) *
- 1.5kg (3lb) granulated sugar (with added pectin if required)
- 6 sterilized jam jars (see page 207)

1 Put some saucers in the freezer. Then tip the fruit into a heavy-bottomed pan and heat for 10–20 minutes until the juices start to run. Add the sugar and stir until dissolved.

2 Whack up the heat until the jam is boiling fast. After 10 minutes' bubbling, drop some jam onto one of the chilled saucers. If the jam wrinkles easily when you push it with your finger, then it is ready; if not, re-test every five minutes until you get a set. Let the jam settle for 15 minutes, then spoon into sterilized jars.

* You can make jam from frozen fruit – just don't wash it before freezing to stop your jam being too runny.

Can I grow my Christmas dinner?

SERVING UP A HOME-GROWN CHRISTMAS DINNER on 25 December is a pinnacle of achievement for any vegetable grower. So how's it done? Can you really settle down to a home-grown feast on the big day?

You can grow almost all the ingredients for your Christmas dinner, as long as you start early – just after the previous Christmas has finished – and plan meticulously to bring everything together on the day.

Growing your own Christmas dinner is cheaper and you know everything on the table is grown with love and without chemicals. Every family's traditional favourites are different, so start by making a wish list of what you'd like on your plate.

Roast potatoes are top of the list for most people, often followed by Brussels sprouts, but you can also add carrots, parsnips, leeks, swede and perhaps red cabbage for braising. Then there's sage and onion for the stuffing, plus other Christmas herbs such as rosemary, thyme and parsley. Don't forget redcurrants for the jelly to accompany the turkey.

Which variety?

Choose varieties carefully: 'Moss Curled' parsley, for example, stays green through winter and a few unusual gourmet veg, such as multicoloured carrots, add extra Christmas bling. For superb roasties, go for floury maincrop potatoes such as 'Cara', 'Picasso' or blight-resistant 'Sarpo Axona'. Grow through summer, then harvest the whole crop and store in sacks until Christmas Day.

Brussels sprout,
Brassica oleracea
Gemmifera Group

AT-A-GLANCE GYO CHRISTMAS TIMETABLE

Winter	• Sow onions indoors. • Plant bare-root redcurrant bushes. • Buy organic maincrop seed potatoes.
Spring	• Sow leeks, parsnips, kale, red cabbage and sprouts. • Plant evergreen herbs. • Plant potatoes. • Transplant onion seedlings outside.
Summer	• Early: Sow carrots, swede, turnips and beetroot. • Mid-: Harvest redcurrants and make redcurrant jelly. • Late: Harvest and dry onions.
Autumn	• Harvest potatoes, dry in the sun for a few hours, then store in hessian or paper sacks. • Dig up carrots, parsnips and other roots and pack in boxes of damp sand. • Lift some leeks and re-bury in loose soil for easy harvest in case it's frosty.
Christmas Day	• Harvest sprouts, sage, rosemary and parsley. • Plunder your stores, pull up leeks and dig root veg as required. • Enjoy the best meal of the year!

Redcurrants,
Ribes rubrum

Parsley,
*Petroselinum
crispum*

Forward planning

Sow faster-growing veg such as carrots, turnips and beetroot until late – early summer is about right – to time it so they reach their peak as the cold weather arrives. You can leave these in the ground until Christmas, but lift some of your crop to store in boxes of damp sand where they will be safe from marauding slugs and mice. Then, on Christmas Day, all you need to do is pop out and pick the sprouts, plus handfuls of aromatic herbs, and then get cooking!

Can I grow my own botanicals for cocktails?

BOTANICALS ARE THE BIGGEST THING in drinks right now. Adding herbs, fruits and flowers to plain old vodka, gin or iced tea transforms drinks into vibrantly flavoured cocktails that taste of nature – and most are from plants you can grow in your garden.

Yuzu,
Citrus x junos

For a good universal botanical, plant rhubarb. It is easy to grow and very prolific. Plant rhubarb in winter, in rich, moisture-retentive soil in sun or partial shade. Then add soft fruits: iced tea or vodka steeped with raspberries, blackberries and cherries is summer in a glass. If you haven't got room for a dedicated berry patch, some varieties can be grown in containers. For tangy, citrusy flavours grow yuzu (*Citrus x junos*), a wild lemon from Japan that makes a tough little shrub hardy to -8°C (18°F) for a well-drained, sunny spot. Its intensely lemony juice is delicious with cucumber, mint, sugar syrup and tonic water.

Herbal botanicals add spicier, aromatic notes. Make a simple syrup by adding a sprig of fresh herb to 100g (3½oz) of sugar and 200ml

RHUBARB GIN RECIPE

You will need
- 1kg (2lb) rhubarb
- 400g (14oz) caster sugar
- 800ml (30fl oz) gin

1 Cut the rhubarb into 3cm (1in) pieces. Place in a jar with the caster sugar (if you wish, add extra botanicals like sliced ginger or raspberries now) and shake. Leave to steep.

2 Next day, add the gin to the jar and shake again. Leave it for a month, stirring every few days. Strain through a muslin-lined sieve into a sterilized bottle (see page 207).

THREE OF THE BEST HOME-GROWN BOTANICAL INFUSIONS

Sloe gin Ripe sloes mellow gin to a rich fruity tipple similar to port. If you can bear it, leave to mature for two years as it gets better with age.

Damson vodka The clean, crisp bite of a good vodka marries perfectly with plummy, fruity damsons (*Prunus domestica* subsp. *insititia*): damson brandy is another sumptuous combination of fruit and alcohol.

Raspberry and mint iced tea Botanicals lift iced tea to new heights: make a pot of tea, pour over raspberries, sugar and mint leaves and leave to cool. Strain, add cold water and serve over ice.

△ Never crush fruit botanicals: leave soft fruits like raspberries whole and for thick-skinned fruits – such as damsons and sloes (see above) from blackthorn (*Prunus spinosa*) – just prick the fruit all over with a pin to release the flavours.

(7fl oz) of water. Heat until the sugar dissolves, then leave to steep for an hour. Add a tablespoon to each glass: try rosemary with lemon juice in gin, or mint and ginger in lemonade.

There's a dazzling range of fruit and herbs you can grow for infusing with alcohol, tea or water. Grow soft fruit for sweetness and herbs for spicy warmth; for a taste of the wild, tuck in a damson tree for small, intensely flavoured plums or blackthorn bushes for an autumn harvest of sloes.

Botanical mixology

There's more to explore, from bergamot leaves (*Monarda didyma*) to lemon balm (*Melissa officinalis*) and even cherry blossom. Partying with home-grown botanicals leaves you feeling better, too: infusing drinks with herbs, leaves and flowers can relieve stress, soothe pain and help you sleep better.

And if you're wondering what to do with the leftovers, booze-infused fruit makes a wickedly indulgent ice cream topping. Or you can turn it into mildly alcoholic jam or even chocolates.

Are big vegetables always better?

RECORD-BREAKING VEG ARE THE STUFF OF LEGENDS: **carrots 5m (16ft) from end to end, onions weighing 8.5kg (18lb 12oz) and massive pumpkins that need a fork lift to move them. It's tempting to measure your own against the champions – but is big always better?**

The size of a vegetable is governed by variety. No matter how good a gardener you are, you'll never persuade an excellent but medium-sized onion such as 'Centurion' to grow as fat as record breakers like 'Kelsae', capable of bulbs with girths measuring over 80cm (3ft). So choose your variety carefully: good choices for mega-veg include 'Atlantic Giant' pumpkins, 'Tropic Giant' cabbages, 'Gigantomo' tomatoes and 'New Red Intermediate' carrots.

Maximize your veg

You'll also get bigger fruits if you remove the competition. Many veg produce lots of smaller fruits, but reduce the quantity and the plant concentrates all its energies on the fruits that remain. Limit the number of trusses on tomatoes to between

Pumpkin,
Cucurbita maxima

It's natural to feel proud when you grow a monster cabbage or a leek as thick as your wrist. But deliberately growing for size requires extra heat, fertilizer and water, with super-sized carbon emissions to match. The end result is often tasteless and tough, whereas smaller veg offer maximum tenderness and flavour for a fraction of the effort and environmental impact.

four and six per plant and once pumpkin or squash fruits start swelling, select the best three or four on each plant and remove the rest for fewer but larger fruits.

Realize the full potential – and size – of all your veg simply by growing them well. Veg grow biggest and best when they bask in sunshine, yet have their roots in rich, damp earth. So make sure the soil is as good as you can get it by keeping it mulched with nutrient-rich, moisture-retentive organic matter such as home-made garden compost or well-rotted farmyard manure. Keep weeds at bay, so your veg don't have to compete with other plants for nutrients or water, and water during dry spells to keep everything growing on strongly.

Don't go too far

Size isn't everything. Many veg have a best-by date: let them grow past this point and skins get tougher, root veg like carrots and beetroot develop woody cores and any flavour is lost. Record-beating champion veg may be impressive, but they're largely inedible – letting a lot of what would otherwise have been good food go to waste.

So pick your veg at their peak, whatever size they are. If in doubt: pick young. Runner beans may grow to impressive lengths, but they're much more delicious when picked small, slender and stringless; beetroots and turnips are best pulled at ping-pong ball size (certainly no bigger than a tennis ball). Carrots are ready once you can feel shoulders 3–4cm (1–1$^{1}/_{2}$in) across just beneath the soil. You may not bag a place in the *Guinness Book of Records*, but you'll be much better fed.

▼ Beetroot are at their most tender pulled at around the size of a ping-pong ball, before they've had time to develop a woody core.

How many squash plants should I grow?

YOU'LL WANT TO MAKE SURE every square foot of ground in your veg patch is working hard to feed you and your family. But how do you know how much space to give each plant – and how do you work out how many you'll need?

Working out how many veg plants you need depends on how many people you're feeding, what you like to eat and how much space you have available.

You'll want to grow more of your favourite veg, so set aside extra space for veg you really like. Then major on compact plants that give you heavy, long-lasting harvests. French and runner beans, cut-and-come-again lettuces and mangetout peas all give great returns for the space they take up. But don't rule out big plants: purple sprouting broccoli, kale and courgettes are so prolific you need only two or three plants for a plentiful supply.

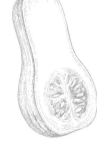

Butternut squash,
Cucurbita moschata

Growing squash vertically
Send squash skywards to fit them into the smallest of gardens. Trailing squashes like butternuts, acorn squashes and 'Black Forest' courgettes scramble readily up sturdy, firmly anchored trellises, archways and obelisks. Plant 1m (3ft) apart and tie in new shoots as the plants grow to create a jungly wall of foliage and fruits.

Squash plants are enormous: the largest grows more than 1.5m (5ft) across. They can also be prolific, so you get a big harvest from each plant: summer squash, like courgettes, produce two or three fruits every few days, while winter squash make three to five – sometimes huge – fruits per plant. This means you don't need many: four squash plants is plenty to feed a family.

Do heirloom varieties taste better?

HERITAGE VARIETIES ARE HAVING SOMETHING OF A REVIVAL. After almost disappearing from cultivation, they're now celebrated for their quirky names, interesting histories – and rich, old-school flavours. But is it true that the veg our ancestors grew really tasted better?

If you grow them well, vegetables tend to taste better home grown. That's because they're harvested when ripe and eaten before flavour compounds break down. But if it's a heritage variety, it's likely to have been bred specifically for its superior flavour.

Although modern varieties have many good qualities, sometimes breeders' priorities are not necessarily things gardeners want. For example, it's more important for carrots to have strong tops for mechanical harvesting than to taste good.

Heritage varieties, though, were largely created by and for gardeners. Head gardeners in walled Victorian estate gardens took pride in developing their own strains of bean, cabbage or tomato, selected for exceptional yields, perfect produce – and mouth-watering flavour.

FIVE HEIRLOOMS TO GROW FOR FLAVOUR

- **Tomato** 'Brandywine'

- **Squash** 'Potimarron'

- **Potato** 'Pink Fir Apple'

- **Lettuce** 'Black Seeded Simpson'

- **Shallot** 'Hative de Niort'

Can I grow my own booze?

HOME BREWING USING FRUIT AND FLOWERS **from the garden has a long history: Julius Caesar found Celts brewing cider from crab apples when he invaded Britain in 55 BC. So is it still just as easy to grow your own alcohol?**

Many of the plants required to grow your own party are hardy and easy-going and blend well into most gardens. Grow just three – elder, hops and apple – and you have all you need to stock your own backyard bar.

Backyard champagne

The easiest backyard booze is brewed from the flowers of hedgerow elder, full of perfume and natural yeast. Elder grows anywhere and is tough and resilient, making a small tree about 4m (13ft) tall that's a magnet for wildlife. The species, *Sambucus nigra*, produces white flowers; pink-flowered 'Black Lace' turns your champagne pink.

ELDERFLOWER CHAMPAGNE RECIPE

You will need
- 25 elderflower heads
- 500g (1lb 2 oz) sugar
- 4 litres (140fl oz) water
- 1¹/₂ tbsp white wine vinegar
- 2 lemons, juiced and peeled

1 Snip off the elderflowers, remove any lurking insects, then drop them into a clean bucket. Add the sugar, water, vinegar, lemon rind and juice, then stir until the sugar has dissolved.

2 Cover with a cloth and leave for six days until it's fizzing nicely.

3 Siphon into sterilized glass bottles (see page 207) and leave for a further five days before drinking chilled.

◀ The champagne will keep fermenting in the bottle, so loosen the bottle top every few days to release the pressure.

Growing hops for beer

Theoretically, you can grow your own beer from scratch, but raising, threshing and malting your own barley is a lot of trouble. So most people stick to growing hops – the flowers that add the bitter flavour to ale.

Hops are easy to grow, making lovely (if rampant) climbers for a garden fence or pergola. Only females produce cones (hops) for flavouring beer, so buy from specialist growers who sell only female plants. You can use flowers from ornamental hops, but you'll get better flavour from specialist beer hop varieties such as 'Fuggle' and 'Prima Donna'. Plant in rich, sunny, free-draining soil; flowers are ready in September once papery dry (they'll also leave a yellow powder on your fingers). Dry in a cool, breezy spot out of direct sunlight. You'll need only a few dried flowers to flavour a keg of beer.

Hop sideshoots and leaves are edible. You can steam the shoots like asparagus and eat young shoots and leaves in salads.

Cider

You can make cider from any apples, but small, hard, bitter cider apples are rich in tannin and have depth of flavour. The best varieties, such as 'Dabinett', 'Slack Ma Girdle' and 'Sheep's Nose' (cider apples major on memorable names), make cider as nuanced and sophisticated as grand cru wine. Roughly chop or crush your apples, then squeeze out the juice with an apple press. Filter through muslin into a clean bucket. Add two teaspoons of yeast, then decant into a demijohn fitted with an airlock. Leave to ferment at 15–20°C (60–68°F) for three or four weeks. Test with a hydrometer: when the reading drops below one your cider is ready.

Apple presses can be expensive but if you have friends with an apple tree or two, you could split the cost and make your cider together.

Do I need a vineyard to grow my own wine?

THE CONNOISSEUR GARDENER'S TIPPLE is home-made wine. Gardeners have been perfecting the art of growing grapes to make wine for thousands of years – but if you fancy filling your wine rack with bottles of Château Homegrown, don't you need a vineyard?

You needn't live somewhere hot to make wine: there are over 700 commercial vineyards in the UK, some as far north as Yorkshire. Many produce award-winning wines rivalling the best in the world. White wines do better in cooler climates, as red grapes struggle to ripen fully.

Give grapevines a sunny spot and well-drained soil. Train them along a wall or pergola, or grow vineyard-style onto freestanding post-and-wire supports, with rows aligned north–south to make the most of the sunshine. Plant in the winter, with 1.2m (4ft) between plants.

WINE GRAPE VARIETIES

You can make wine from dessert grapes, but smaller, thick-skinned wine grapes have richer flavours.

White
'Seyval Blanc' Great all-rounder white wine grape, super reliable and high yielding; 'Sauvignon Blanc' Classic fruity white but needs sun, so more of a gamble; 'Gewürztraminer' Pink-skinned grape from Alsace, which makes spicy golden wine.

Red and rosé
'Pinot Noir' Superb red wine grape that performs fairly well even in cooler areas; 'Dornfelder' German grape varieties suit most climates – this one ripens fully even in the UK.

Pruning

Prune vines in midwinter. For garden grapes, select two or three main stems for your framework, then cut sideshoots back to two buds from these stems each year.

For freestanding vines use the Guyot system. Prune back the main stem to three strong buds near the lowest wire. Then during the summer, train one stem to each side with the third tied in vertically. Tie sideshoots from the two arms upwards – these produce your fruit. Pinch out any sideshoots from the central vertical stem to one leaf during summer, then remove fruited side arms and cut back the central stem to three buds in winter. These buds become next year's framework.

Vegetable wines

It's not all grapes. You can make wine from elderberries, blackberries, gooseberries or strawberries. And parsnip wine, aged for a few years, can rival the best medium-dry white.

The process is essentially the same: add 5 litres (1 gallon) of boiling water to about 3kg (7lb) of fruit – or chop 3kg (7lb) of parsnips and boil until soft – then strain and add sugar and yeast before fermenting. Home-made wines have a reputation for being dodgy, but that's usually because they're drunk too soon: age wines for at least a couple of years if you want to enjoy them at their fruity, full-bodied best.

A One well-grown vine produces enough grapes to make about three bottles of wine – so if you're just making home-grown wine as a hobby, you only need a couple of grapevines in the garden or a few rows on the allotment.

WINE RECIPE

You will need
- 6–7kg (13–15lb) grapes for 4–5 litres (1 gallon) wine
- 900g (2lb) granulated sugar
- 1 tsp wine yeast

1 Crush the grapes with a potato masher. Strain through muslin into a sterilized bucket. Cover with a cloth and leave for 24 hours.

2 Add the sugar and wine yeast. Stir daily for eight days.

3 Strain the wine into a sterilized demijohn, seal and leave for eight weeks. Pour the wine off carefully, leaving the sediment behind, and bottle.

Do I have to grow more than one apple tree to get a crop?

APPLE BLOSSOM MUST BE POLLINATED if it's to produce fruit and usually that pollen must come from a different apple tree. So do you always have to find enough room for two apple trees to guarantee a good crop?

When you buy an apple tree you'll find it's assigned a pollination group. Each group contains all the varieties that flower at roughly the same time, so can cross-pollinate each other: plant two different varieties of apple from the same group and you can rely on a good harvest (two trees of the same variety won't cross-pollinate each other). You'll find compatible varieties listed in their pollination groups on the RHS website.

Self-fertile varieties

There is also a small – but useful – group of self-fertile apple varieties, such as 'Braeburn' and 'Granny Smith', which are able to produce fruit without a partner. They're a very good choice if you only have room for one tree, although you will still get more fruit if you can plant another compatible variety nearby.

A better way around the problem is to plant a crab apple tree. These

Planting two apple trees of different but compatible varieties guarantees the best possible level of pollination – and therefore fruit set – each year. But if your garden is small, or you only want one tree, there are ways around this. In city gardens there's often another tree growing nearby. Self-pollinating varieties can produce fruit without a partner.

HOW DOES POLLINATION WORK?

All fruiting plants rely on flying insects to transfer pollen from the anther of a male flower to the stigma of a female flower, fertilizing it so it swells into a fruit. Sometimes, pollen can transfer between flowers on the same tree (self-fertility); but more often, you need a bee to bring pollen from flowers open at the same time on another apple tree growing within about 18m (60ft) – the optimum flying distance for bees.

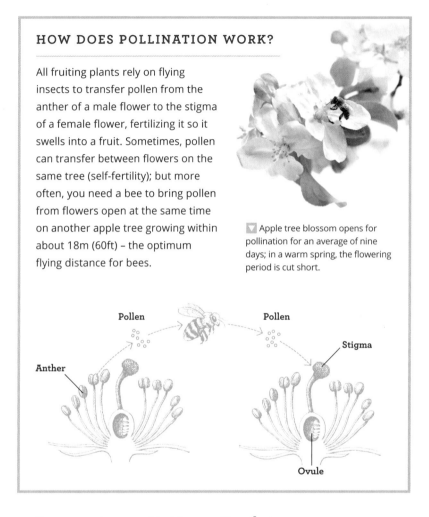

▼ Apple tree blossom opens for pollination for an average of nine days; in a warm spring, the flowering period is cut short.

Pollen

Pollen

Stigma

Anther

Ovule

small, ornamental trees are ideal for compact gardens and produce lots of pollen over a long period of time, pollinating a wide range of apple trees. Choose white-flowered varieties like 'John Downie' or 'Evereste' rather than those with red or pink flowers to cross-pollinate apples, as bees tend to visit flowers of the same colour.

Family trees

It's possible to graft several varieties of fruit tree onto the same roots, producing 'family' apple trees in which two or three compatible types of apple grow on the same trunk. This is useful when you only have room for one tree, but they can grow unevenly and need careful management to stop a dominant variety taking over.

Can I grow lemons in a cold climate?

As CLIMATE CHANGE WARMS OUR SUMMERS, it's tempting to try growing fruit and veg outside their comfort zones. But are we asking for trouble by planting lemons – used to basking in Mediterranean sun – in gardens verging on the chilly side?

Many citrus are surprisingly tolerant of cold. Meyer lemons, Seville oranges and kumquats even cope with short bouts of frost, as long as they're dry at the roots – cold plus soggy compost is a fatal combination.

Grow lemons in roomy (45–60cm/ 1½–2ft) terracotta pots, kept outside from early summer to mid-autumn. Water with rainwater and feed with liquid seaweed all year round.

Winter quarters need only be an unheated greenhouse or conservatory. Lemon trees also hate sudden temperature changes, so acclimatize over a period of at least two weeks.

Lemon substitutes for colder gardens

If you can't overwinter a lemon tree, grow yuzu (*Citrus* x *junos*) instead. This wild lemon has an intense, zesty flavour and can tolerate frosts down to -8°C (18°F). Even hardier is the thorny Japanese bitter orange (*Citrus trifoliata*). The mandarin-sized fruit are too sour to eat raw, but delicious cooked: they make superb marmalade.

It's true that if you garden in, say, mild-but-cool southern England your lemon is unlikely to grow into the kind of flourishing, fruit-laden, full-sized tree you'd find in the baking sunshine of Sicily. But that doesn't mean you can't have home-grown lemons. Choose cold-tolerant varieties and grow in containers you can move indoors through the winter, and you too can pick your own slice of sunshine.

Will my olive tree grow olives?

THINK OF OLIVE TREES and you're probably picturing sun-drenched hillsides in Greece and Italy. In fact, they're surprisingly hardy, tolerating frosts to -12°C (10°F), and grow outdoors all year round, even in cool climates. Once mature, three to five years after planting, they also start fruiting.

Olives need a very long, hot summer to develop fruit fully; even in the Mediterranean the harvest isn't until late autumn. But heatwaves induced by climate change are improving the odds of a ripe olive harvest by the year: in fact, Britain now has a commercial olive grove, planted in Kent.

Boost your chances of ripe olives by buying named, self-fertile varieties known to fruit early, such as 'Frantoio', 'Arbequina' or 'Picual'. Olives grown in containers often fruit better, too. Give your olive tree the sunniest spot you can, water well if it's dry in spring when flower buds are forming, and feed regularly with liquid comfrey feed (see page 124) throughout summer. Pick the fruit slightly unripe, as green olives, in mid-autumn; or hold out for black olives, which have more oil and a subtler, less bitter flavour, from late autumn onwards.

HOW TO BRINE OLIVES

Freshly picked olives are bitter and must be brined to bring out their flavours.

- Slit each olive down one side, then soak in water for two weeks, changing the water every day.

- Make a brine, dissolving 100g of salt per 1 litre (4oz per 40fl oz) of water, and soak the olives in this for a couple of days.

- Rinse the olives in fresh water, then soak in white vinegar for six hours.

- Pack into clean jars and cover in sunflower oil, adding garlic, herbs or chilli to taste. Your olives will be ready to enjoy in about two weeks.

Do edible flowers actually taste of anything?

A SPRINKLE OF EDIBLE FLOWERS makes even the plainest cake Instagrammable. Pansies, marigolds, lavender and borage flowers are popping up on patisserie, in cocktails, and scattered over salads. But do all those photogenic petals actually add anything to the flavour?

You don't always want edible flowers to have much flavour. In fact, it's precisely because pansies, primroses and pinks don't taste of much that they work so well as decorations, as they don't overwhelm the flavour of the cake itself.

Some have a flavour close to perfume: lavender infuses biscuits with the same aroma as the flowers, while rose petals from a highly scented variety like the apothecary's rose (*Rosa gallica* var. *officinalis*) lift jellies or panna cotta to fragrant sophistication.

Strong flavours for salads

Flowers with the strongest flavours work brilliantly in salads. Chive flowers add an oniony tang and the peppery bite of rocket flowers is set off beautifully with a dash of sweet nectar. A few crisp daylily buds add a fresh, lettuce-like flavour and brilliant yellow brassica flowers have a tender, delicate flavour like young calabrese.

HOW TO MAKE EDIBLE FLOWER ICE CUBES

Suspend flowers in ice cubes to give cocktails an elegant, home-grown twist.

• Half-fill your ice cube trays with water.

• Place a single borage, lavender or pansy flower in each compartment.

• Pop the trays in the freezer for a few hours.

• Top up with more water so the flowers are suspended within the cube. Refreeze.

• Pop a cube or two in each drink; as they melt, the flower is released.

FIVE FLOWERS FOR FLAVOUR

Scented-leaved pelargonium
The flowers borrow their flavours
from the scented leaves, which
range from peppermint to citrus.

Nasturtium Both flowers and
leaves are peppery and delicious
in salads (below).

Radish The flowers are sweet
with a peppery twist (above),
followed by equally delicious
green seed pods.

Sunflower Use the crunchy
petals like brightly coloured
salad leaves: they taste faintly
of sunflower seeds.

Lavender Infuse its sweet,
fragrant flavour into sugar,
biscuits and cakes.

How to harvest edible flowers

Pick early in the morning when flowers
are full of moisture, just as they're
about to open – they'll open further
after picking. Don't wash them:
instead, pick over them carefully to
remove stalks and any damaged petals.
Keep them in the fridge in an airtight
container until you need them.

Always harvest your own flowers
rather than eating blooms from
bought-in bouquets, which may have
been sprayed with chemicals.

Until quite recently, flowers
were for the bees. But now
we're discovering a scattering
of petals turns food and drink
into works of art. Most are just
there to look pretty, but some
– especially the flowers of
herbs and vegetables – have a
distinctive flavour. Grow them
alongside your veg to add
gorgeous colour – they may
also attract beneficial insects.

Can I grow plants from kitchen scraps?

LOW-IMPACT GARDENING is all about making good use of what's around you. Rather than spending a fortune shopping for seeds, tubers and bulbs, could you turn the leftover trimmings from last night's supper into new crops?

Potato,
Solanum tuberosum

Potatoes

Plant whole – or cut up – potatoes. You can also regrow potatoes from peelings as long as they have at least one bud (like a tiny indented dot). Dry cut surfaces for a day or two to seal them before you plant.

Sweet potatoes

Place tubers in water, tapered end down (the larger end, with eyes, is where shoots emerge). Twist the shoots off at 12–15cm (4–6in) long and pop into another jar of water to root, then pot up and grow on.

Veg you can regrow from scraps include tubers, some leafy veg, alliums (the onion family) and seedy veg like tomatoes and chillies. Tubers from shops have often been sprayed with anti-sprouting agent to stop them growing. Wash thoroughly to remove the worst, or buy organic.

Bear in mind that veg intended for eating isn't as carefully vetted for plant viruses and other diseases as that raised for planting in gardens – so growing from scraps is always riskier, but worth a try.

Sweet potato,
Ipomoea batatas

When we're preparing vegetables to eat, we tend to reject and trim off the plant's original growing points: skins with embryonic buds, root plates and seeds. Give these scraps soil, water and a little warmth and they burst into life again, sprouting into new plants. It's fun, it's free – and you can stock a whole veg garden from the contents of your fridge.

 Garlic needs a spell of cold to split into cloves, so plant your kitchen-scrap garlic cloves outside in early winter.

Lemongrass

Check stems are whole, with slightly woody bases, then stand in a glass of water. Be patient as rooting can take weeks: pot up, protect from frost and your lemongrass clump will last for years.

Celery

Cut stems off a head of celery, 5–8cm (2–3in) above the base, and stand the stump in water. Within a week or so you should have a tuft of leaves and embryonic roots. Pot up in peat-free compost: harvest stems and leaves as required.

Garlic

Shop-bought garlic bulbs grow just as easily as those from the garden centre. Break the bulb into cloves and plant the largest into rich, free-draining soil 15cm (6in) apart, pointy end up and with the tips 2–3cm (^{3}/$_4$–1in) beneath the surface.

Once your celery has begun to sprout, plant it out straightaway to prevent the outer stalk from rotting. You'll be harvesting in around four months' time.

What's the most environmentally friendly way to grow new plants?

AS GARDENERS, WE'VE GOT LOTS OF CHOICE when it comes to getting our hands on new plants: we can buy them from the garden centre in every size, from plug plants to small trees, or raise our own from seed, cuttings and divisions. But which way is kindest to the planet?

The greenest plants are grown in home-made compost, in wooden seedtrays and biodegradable pots, from seed and cuttings collected from your own plants or those growing in the gardens of friends or family.

It's amazingly easy to produce new plants from scratch. Blackcurrants, gooseberries and redcurrants root readily from hardwood cuttings. Dig up and replant raspberry suckers and rooted strawberry runners, and split rhubarb clumps into new crowns while dormant. In spring, take softwood cuttings of evergreen herbs and divide clump-forming mint, chives and oregano.

Save your own seed for day-to-day veg such as lettuces, tomatoes and beans, but if you want to try new varieties buying seed is relatively

◀ Repurpose cardboard egg boxes to make sowing modules; simply break apart and bury along with the seedlings.

low-impact as long as you source it from local, organic producers who collect their own seed.

Commercially produced, ready-grown plants have the highest environmental price tag, with transport, peat-based compost and pesticides all adding to the cost. Keep the impact down by buying as locally as possible, from organic growers who use peat-free compost. Buy plants young, so they've taken up fewer resources, and not too many – as long as the variety isn't protected by plant breeder's rights, you can often take cuttings to get more. And look for bare-root plants, sold from autumn until early spring. These are dug up straight from the field to send to you, at just the right time for planting, and there's now an increasingly good range available as gardeners look for more eco-friendly plant-buying solutions.

The more plants you produce at home, the greener your garden. So seeds, cuttings and divisions you've collected win hands down. They take longer, though, and the choice is more limited. If you do buy seeds or plants, then buy local organic ones (to avoid pesticides) and make sure they've been grown in peat-free compost.

SOW SEED NATURE'S WAY

Go even greener than sowing your own seed – and let your plants do it themselves. Leave carrots, beetroot, chard, rocket, corn salad, lettuce – as well as herbs like chervil and fennel – in the ground till they flower and run to seed naturally. The following spring look for little clusters of seedlings you can carefully transplant to where you want them to grow.

Do I really have to sow all my vegetables from seed each year?

VEG GROWERS ARE UNUSUAL in that they sow almost a complete garden, from scratch, every year. Though sowing seed is hugely exciting and a lot of fun, it's also a fair bit of work, especially if you have a whole allotment or a large veg patch to fill. So is there an easier way of doing it?

Perennials – plants that come back year after year – save you loads of time, and growing for the long haul is climate-friendly too. Perennial plants sequester more carbon than annuals: they keep soil undisturbed and take up fewer resources like compost, fertilizer and water.

In fact, you can plant much of your veg garden once and harvest for years. As well as long-lived fruit and herbs, include a bed of asparagus for tender spears each spring for decades. A clump of Jerusalem artichokes keeps you in knobbly winter tubers indefinitely, too.

Extend the life of annuals

Many familiar crops we know as annuals are really short-lived perennials. Chilli peppers often survive winter in a frost-free greenhouse: 'Rocoto' (*Capsicum pubescens*) and 'Aji' (*Capsicum baccatum*) chillies are very cold tolerant and grow bigger and better with each year.

There's really no need to resow kale, spinach-like chard or sprouting broccoli every year, either. Special

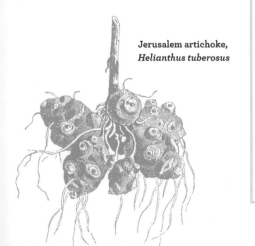

Jerusalem artichoke,
Helianthus tuberosus

Many of the vegetables we eat such as lettuces and sweetcorn are true annuals; others, like tomatoes and courgettes, won't survive the cold weather, so you do have to resow these each spring. But a surprising number are actually short-lived perennials. The more perennial veg you grow, the fewer seeds you have to sow and the easier your veg-growing life becomes.

Chard, *Beta vulgaris*
subsp. *cicla* var.
flavescens

perennial varieties of kale crop steadily for about five years, after which you can take cuttings to keep your supply going. Or just keep any variety of kale, chard or sprouting broccoli going season after season by cutting back hard in spring as plants start to flower. They'll resprout from the stumps and give you another year's harvest. At the end of four or five years of this, start again in a new part of the plot to avoid the buildup of pests and diseases.

FIVE HARDY PERENNIAL VEGETABLES TO TRY

Kale 'Daubenton's' Among the best perennial kales, making a tall (1.5m/5ft), gawky brassica lush with leaves for up to five years. It doesn't set viable seed, so propagate from cuttings.

Leek 'Babington's' Harvest just the tops of these leeks, cutting about 5cm (2in) above soil level, and the stump resprouts. The whole plant dies back naturally in summer, returning in autumn to do it all over again.

Caucasian spinach Enthusiastic climber and tasty perennial spinach substitute, happy in sun or shade: pick leaves young and tender.

Skirret Tudorbethan vegetable that grows into clumps of sweet, skinny roots: leave some in the ground to continue to grow each time you harvest.

Potato bean Small but tasty American groundnut that forms underground tubers which serve as a good alternatives to potatoes, floury in texture and with a bean-like flavour.

What can I pick from my veg garden in winter?

A WELL-PLANTED VEG PATCH is a powerhouse of productivity in summer – there's so much to pick, you're spoiled for choice. But what if you want that home-grown flavour all year round? Can you still keep the harvest going in the depths of winter?

FIVE WINTER VEG TO TRY

Winter kale Varieties like 'Dwarf Green Curled' and 'Redbor' shrug off winter weather: harvest leaves young, no more than 15cm (6in) long.

Parsnips Sow direct in late spring (seeds take up to a month to germinate) and simply leave to grow: roots keep well in the ground until you're ready to harvest.

Leeks Sow in pots and grow on to 20cm (8in) high before transplanting outside; varieties like 'Musselburgh' withstand any amount of cold.

Kalettes A cross between Brussels sprouts and kale and super easy to grow, with stems covered in mini-cabbages to pick throughout winter.

Purple sprouting broccoli Plants are prolific, producing delicious sprigs of purple florets continuously for weeks; plant early- and late-maturing varieties to pick from late autumn until spring.

Parsnip,
Pastinaca sativa

Purple sprouting broccoli,
Brassica oleracea Italica Group

A well-stocked winter veg garden is all about timing. Many winter crops take almost a year to reach harvesting size – so sow winter brassicas, parsnips, celeriac, leeks and maincrop carrots in late spring to give them enough time to mature.

Other winter crops are just fast-growing summer veg sown late, to reach harvesting size as winter hits: sow batches of early (i.e. fast maturing) carrots, beetroots and turnips in midsummer and they are ready to eat through late autumn and early winter.

Midsummer is also sowing time for winter-hardy versions of summer leaves, including winter lettuces, white-stemmed chard and 'Giant Winter' spinach. Add short-day-length crops like mizuna, pak choi and chicory to your greenhouse borders or outside under cloches for spicy, flavour-filled salads all winter long.

LOOKING AFTER THE WINTER VEG GARDEN

- Mulch in autumn, tucking soil safely beneath an insulating blanket of organic matter.

- Stake tall plants like Brussels sprouts, so winter gales can't blow them over.

- Lay straw around parsnips and leeks to stop soil freezing.

- Hoe off winter weeds.

- Cover brassicas with insect-proof mesh or plastic-free calico to keep off pigeons.

Pak choi, *Brassica rapa* Chinensis Group

Vegetables at their best in winter are among the finest you can grow: hearty brassicas, buttery leeks and parsnips, sweet maincrop carrots, hardy winter greens, and aromatic swedes and celeriac all provide the warming, comforting foods you want when it's cold and bleak outside.

Can I grow my morning cuppa?

As any Brit will tell you, everything feels better after a nice cup of tea. But your daily cuppa is almost certainly imported and teabags often contain environmentally damaging plastic polymers. So can you cut the environmental cost of your morning brew by growing your own instead?

Chinese camellia,
Camellia sinensis

Black tea is made from the leaves and shoot tips of the Chinese camellia (*Camellia sinensis*), an evergreen shrub that survives all but the hardest winters outside and will even grow in roomy containers. So there's no reason why you shouldn't grow your own cuppa – in fact, the UK already has several commercial tea plantations, one as far north as Scotland!

First, make sure you have the right type of camellia. Garden camellias grown for their showy spring flowers are usually cultivars of *Camellia japonica* or *C. sasanqua*. The tea camellia, *C. sinensis*, is closely related but has narrower leaves and pure white, lightly scented flowers in autumn.

Growing tea camellias

Like all camellias, the tea camellia grows best in acidic to neutral soil. You can do a soil test with an inexpensive kit to check how acidic your soil is, or simply look at nearby plants: if rhododendrons grow happily where you are, you'll probably be able to grow tea plants. If you garden on more alkaline soil, plant in a roomy container instead, using peat-free ericaceous (acidic) potting compost.

HOW TO MAKE TEA

Tea is made from young shoot tips, picked as two leaves and a bud. A small handful of fresh shoot tips makes one cup of tea.

Green tea, widely drunk in Asia, is the quickest to make: it's light-coloured and delicately flavoured, with lower caffeine levels. Black tea takes longer to process but tastes stronger, with the red-brown colouring more familiar to European tea drinkers.

Green tea Spread shoot tips out to wither for 4–8 hours. Then steam for a minute, rinse under cold water and mash by wrapping them in a cloth and rolling against a hard surface, breaking up the ball and re-rolling until juice squeezes out. Dry in a low oven 80–100°C (175–210°F) for 10 minutes until crispy.

Black tea Spread shoot tips out to wither for 12–24 hours, then roll the leaves as for green tea. Spread the wet, crushed leaves somewhere warm for another 4–8 hours until they've turned brassy orange. Dry at 100–110°C (210–230°F) for 15 minutes, then turn the oven down to 80°C (175°F) and dry for a further 10 minutes until crispy and black.

Home-grown tea keeps for up to 12 months in an airtight container.

Choose a sheltered spot in sun or partial shade, and water well in dry spells. Mulch generously in autumn or spring, and feed plants in pots regularly during the growing season using feed formulated for citrus plants. Harvest lightly in the first year, but after that you can pick tea several times during the season.

▶ Freshly made, home-grown tea is thought to contain higher levels of antioxidants – so it's good for you, too.

Which home-grown herbs make the best tea?

HERBAL TEAS DISTIL THE FRAGRANCES AND FLAVOURS of herbs into soothing hot drinks – the ideal pick-me-up at the end of a long day. So which herbs are best for making herbal tea – and how do you do it?

Corn mint,
Mentha arvensis

Plant a well-stocked herbal tea garden and you can enjoy a different herbal tea every day. Herbal teas are naturally caffeine-free, and some help you feel better: mint teas are great for settling indigestion, while sage tea soothes a sore throat.

Where to grow
Tea herbs tend to be Mediterranean plants packed with fragrant essential oils, at their best basking in sunshine. So choose a suntrap for your tea garden and gritty, free-draining soil. Most tea herbs also grow well in containers; in fact, mint is better behaved when in a pot as it tends to spread rampantly in the garden.

Know what you're growing
Choose varieties carefully as common names can be confusing. Classic chamomile tea, for example, is made with annual German chamomile (*Matricaria recutita*); one teaspoon of dried flowers or two teaspoons of fresh makes a stress-busting drink. You can also make tea from perennial Roman chamomile (*Chamaemelum nobile*)

FIVE-MINUTE HERBAL TEA

This tea takes no longer to brew than your regular cuppa.

• Pick a 10cm (4in)-long sprig of your favourite herb, choosing a young, fresh, leafy stem.

• Swish gently in cold water, then pop in a mug.

• Pour boiling water over the top and leave to steep for 5 minutes.

• Remove the sprig from your mug and enjoy!

When you grow your own herbs you can get adventurous. As well as standard peppermint and chamomile tea, branch out and try different flavours of mint, or refreshing citrusy lemon verbena tea. Sage, thyme and echinacea flowers make great pick-me-up brews when you're under the weather, while fennel tea tastes of liquorice.

but its relaxing properties aren't as strong, and the flavour is milder.

Home-grown herbs are brewed freshly picked, while essential oils are at their best: they need no processing (or plastic packaging) and make a stronger, fresher-tasting tea. Dry surplus chamomile flowers and freeze mint leaves (strip from the stalks, wash, then pack into sealed plastic bags), to enjoy home-grown herbal tea right through the year.

German chamomile,
Matricaria recutita

HERBS FOR A HERBAL TEA GARDEN

- Moroccan mint (*Mentha spicata* var. *crispa* 'Moroccan') for gourmet mint tea.

- Chamomile (*Matricaria recutita*) for a bedtime drink brewed from flowers.

- Chocolate mint (*Mentha × piperita* f. *citrata* 'Chocolate') tastes of after-dinner mints.

- Echinacea (*Echinacea purpurea*) flower petals make a health-boosting tea.

- Fennel (*Foeniculum vulgare*) seeds make liquorice-flavoured tea.

- Lemon verbena (*Aloysia triphylla*) makes an intensely citrusy tea.

- Lemon balm (*Melissa officinalis*) is also lemony and very easy to grow.

- Rosemary (*Salvia rosmarinus*) tea is said to help with concentration.

- Sage (*Salvia officinalis*) brews a soothing tea for sore throats.

- Thyme (*Thymus officinalis*) for a restorative, refreshing tea.

Is it worth growing grains in your garden?

WE CAN GROW MOST EVERYDAY FOOD in the garden, so why not the main ingredient for bread? You don't often find cereals growing in veg plots, so does this mean they're not worth the effort?

Sow cereal grains in spring for an autumn crop: scatter seeds sparingly across damp ground and rake in. Plants turn golden brown in late summer; test kernels – once they're hard, they're ready.

Quinoa and amaranth grow 1–2m (3–6½ft) tall and produce about 450g (1lb) gluten-free, couscous-like seeds per ten plants; quinoa is the easier choice for cooler climates. Sow direct in late spring, thinning seedlings to 30cm (12in) apart.

Harvest big, plume-like quinoa seedheads once leaves turn yellow. Dry the seedheads for a few days, place in a pillowcase and beat against a wall to release seeds plus debris. Pick out larger bits by hand, then pass the rest through a 5mm (¼in) mesh sieve. Finally, winnow by pouring the remaining seed-and-fluff mix from one bucket to another in a gentle breeze, so the fluff blows away, leaving only clean seed. Store the seed in jars. Before cooking, soak overnight, then rinse. Harvest amaranth when seeds fall from flowerheads easily when rubbed: the seeds don't need soaking and are ready to cook straightaway.

It's easy to grow traditional grains like wheat, barley and oats at home. But you need a lot of garden: 3sq m (32sq ft) of wheat produces just two loaves of bread. So it's an interesting experiment. You'll get a better food supply from rice-like 'grains' (actually seeds) such as quinoa and amaranth, with higher yields for smaller plots.

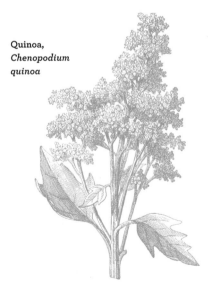

Quinoa,
*Chenopodium
quinoa*

Is growing veg good for the environment?

IF YOU GROW YOUR OWN VEG, **you'll already know how great it tastes. It's also miles cheaper and a lot more fun than a trip to the supermarket. But is it better for the environment, too?**

Any vegetables you grow at home reduce your reliance on commercially produced food. But growing those with a high commercial carbon footprint bring the biggest returns for the environment. Home-grown food follows the seasons, meaning you won't be flying grapes halfway across the world so you can eat them in winter. And salad leaves grown in containers need never be bagged in plastic or washed in chlorine to keep them fresh.

△ In the UK, about 40 percent of bagged baby-leaf salads ends up in the bin: grow your own and it's less likely to go to waste.

Benefits of growing your own

When you grow veg at home you waste less food as you pick only what you need, and you know just how much effort has gone into each carrot – so you don't mind if they're wonky. It's likely that when your veg is plentiful, free and tastes great, you'll eat more plants and less high-carbon meat.

How you do it matters, though. Grow in containers using bought-in multipurpose compost and the carbon

Growing your own food is one of the most effective ways to cut your carbon footprint – right up there with planting trees or driving an electric car. Farming, plus packaging, transporting and selling food in shops accounts for around a quarter of all carbon emissions. Grow your own and for fresh produce at least that falls to almost zero.

saving is negligible: use home-made potting compost (see page 156) and you start to win again. In fact, as long as you grow sustainably, starting a veg garden could be the greenest thing you ever do.

Can I grow my own beanpoles?

ONE VISIT TO A GARDEN CENTRE is enough to tell you that gardeners need an awful lot of stuff. You can spend a fortune buying everything, from string and fertilizers to labels and supports for your plants – but is there a more sustainable way to supply yourself with gardening gear?

Coppiced hazel makes the best beanpoles, producing ramrod-straight, 2m (6½ft) stems to support climbing plants. Ideally, plant three common hazels (*Corylus avellana*) and coppice one each year, for poles at an ideal 3–5cm (1–2in) in diameter. In smaller gardens, just plant one and cut a third of the stems each year.

Make wigwams by tying together the tops of hazel poles, then use whippy young willow or dogwood stems to weave through and strengthen the uprights. Dogwood and willow also make lovely trellis lashed together and fixed to a fence – don't stick them in the ground, though, as (unlike hazel) they will readily take root.

More home-made gear

Cut a leaf of New Zealand flax (*Phormium tenax*) and strip it into tough strands of fibrous 'string' for tying in plants. Split bamboo canes lengthways to make dibbers and plant labels. Grow yourself a comfrey patch for home-made fertilizer (see page 124). You may never need to visit a garden centre again.

Lash 2.4m (8ft)-tall hazel beanpoles together to make an A-frame support strong enough to hold fully laden runner bean plants.

Plant supports such as beanpoles are particularly easy to grow yourself: there's room for hazel, dogwood and willow even in smaller gardens. You can make other garden sundries from materials harvested from garden plants, too, from string to plant labels. They're free, you never run out, and it's kinder to the environment as well.

MUST-HAVE PLANTS FOR GARDEN SUNDRIES

Hazel (*Corylus avellana*) For beanpoles, pea sticks, edging and hurdles. Small, easy-going tree that grows almost anywhere. Give it two years to establish, then harvest stems every three years, cutting to 5cm (2in) above ground in early spring.

New Zealand flax (*Phormium tenax*) For string and pea netting (see opposite). Large, evergreen, strappy foliage plant available in multiple colours. Plant in open ground or in containers in either sun or partial shade, and in free-draining soil.

Dogwood (*Cornus alba*) For light plant supports and weaving through wigwams. Plant in the garden or in roomy pots in a sunny spot. Harvest stems annually, cutting them back to 5cm (2in) above ground level each spring.

Golden willow,
Salix alba var.
vitellina

Golden willow (*Salix alba* var. *vitellina*) For fencing, edging and weaving through wigwams. Plant in damp soil in sun or partial shade, and harvest as for dogwood. Cut stems every two years for thicker poles to use in trellis making. Keep newly cut willow stems flexible after cutting by dunking them in a pond until you need them.

Bamboo For plant supports, trellis, plant labels and dibbers. Fast-growing, architectural plant that grows in any moist, well-drained soil. Choose a less invasive, clump-forming variety like *Fargesia* or grow in roomy containers to stop it spreading.

Dogwood,
Cornus alba

What's a forest garden?

NEW IDEAS ABOUT HOW TO GROW FOOD are overturning many traditional practices in favour of more environmentally friendly techniques which harness the power of nature to help us feed ourselves. One that's generated lots of interest lately is forest gardening – so what's it all about?

Forest gardens are planted in 'layers' of perennial plants that work together and support each other, just as they would in nature. They can be as small as a single 'guild' (see page 136) of complementary plants grouped around one fruit tree, or you can plant your whole garden as edible woodland.

Forest gardens are edible ecosystems – veg patches planted just like a woodland to mimic nature's way of growing food. They're permanently planted, highly productive and low maintenance, giving you a generous harvest of fruits, nuts, leafy greens and herbs with a fraction of the work required to look after a conventional veg plot.

Forest garden layers

Start by planting the canopy layer of fruit and nut trees. Then add a lower-growing layer of currants and ornamental shrubs with edible berries like chokeberry (*Aronia*) and autumn olive (*Elaeagnus umbellata*). Lower layers are made up of leafy veg and herbs. Many perennial vegetables (see page 42) and shade-loving annual crops – like lettuce and spinach – thrive in forest gardens. Finally, living mulches, such as butternut squash, strawberries or clover, cover the

▶ Forest gardens are planted to make the most of the planting area, with different height plants, or layers, making the most of the light and ground covered. 1. Canopy 2. Shrub layer 3. Understorey perennials 4. Ground cover.

PLANTS FOR FOREST GARDENS

Canopy layer Sweet chestnut
(*Castanea sativa*), filbert (*Corylus maxima*), almond, apple, pear

Shrub layer Serviceberry
(*Amelanchier*, right), Sichuan
pepper (*Zanthoxylum simulans*),
blackcurrant, gooseberry (*Ribes uva-crispa*), Japanese bitter
orange (*Citrus trifoliata*)

Understorey perennials Spinach,
kale, lettuce, mizuna, daylilies
(for edible flower buds), parsley,
lemon balm, chicory, mint

Ground cover Alpine strawberry
(*Fragaria vesca*, left), Chinese
bramble (*Rubus tricolor*)

ground, locking in moisture and keeping out weeds.

One drawback of forest gardening is that many of our favourite foods need more sunlight than is found on the woodland floor. So to grow courgettes, sweetcorn or climbing beans you'll need to create open, sunny areas – or keep a conventional veg patch alongside your forest garden. Forest gardening does not require much maintenance as it harnesses natural processes to do the work for you. Include at least one legume such as broom (*Cytisus scoparius*) or shrub lupins (*Lupinus arboreus*) to 'fix' nitrogen from the air as natural

fertilizer. Let leaves and prunings lie where they fall, decomposing to feed the soil. Birds and predatory insects drawn in by flowering herbs like tansy protect plants from pests. Once established, your garden should look after itself – while providing you with an endless harvest of forever food.

Tansy, *Tanacetum vulgare*

Which veg are easiest to grow in an eco-friendly way?

GROWING VEG SUSTAINABLY MEANS USING RESOURCES with care, whether you're watering wisely, doing without artificial fertilizers or ditching the pesticides. But which vegetables cope best with a natural approach?

Happily, veg that perform well in eco-friendly veg patches tend to be those that require least effort to grow. Look for drought-tolerant, resilient veg you won't have to water. Naturally pest and disease-resistant varieties are able to protect themselves. Grow veg that are at home in your climate, and go for reliable, high-yielding varieties to get the best return for the fewest resources.

Environmentally friendly veg gardens major on vigorous, naturally healthy veg that romp away the moment they're in the ground, producing plentiful food for months without requiring any cosseting.

When choosing varieties, look for 'AGM' after the name (see page 16). Varieties bred to be naturally resistant to pests and diseases insure you against losses without having to resort to pesticides. Grow crops slugs dislike, such as parsnips, rocket and red-leaved lettuces, and your harvests will be intact, without the need for pellets.

Consider your conditions

It helps if the vegetables you grow prefer the climate where you live. Greenhouses let you enjoy heat-loving crops such as chillies, aubergines and melons – but growing under glass can be intensive, high-input gardening. So it's usually greener to grow outside.

Slugs are drawn to sweeter yellow and green lettuces, but generally leave more savoury, red-coloured varieties alone.

Legumes – from the pea and bean family – feed themselves by drawing nitrogen from the air, acting as natural fertilizer for crops growing nearby. Drought-tolerant chard grows through dry spells with minimal extra watering and makes a better choice than notoriously thirsty spinach. Most root veg, plus leeks and brassicas – except cauliflowers – don't need much extra watering. In fact, choosing veg that works in harmony with nature means most of the work is done for you, so all you have to do is pick the harvest.

ECO-FRIENDLY VEGETABLES TO GROW IN YOUR GARDEN

Runner beans
High-yielding and nitrogen-fixing (hybrids like 'Moonlight' are also drought-tolerant). Sow in loo roll inners in late spring for planting out in early summer at the feet of sturdy hazel beanpole wigwams.

Runner bean, *Phaseolus coccineus*

Kale
High-yielding, drought-tolerant and relatively unattractive to pests. Sow seed into newspaper modules in late spring, then plant out under insect-proof mesh in early summer.

Beetroot
High-yielding, drought-tolerant and with few pests or diseases. Sow direct into shallow drills at regular intervals from early spring for a constant supply. Pick leaves sparingly for salads, then pull roots at tennis ball size.

Chard
High-yielding and very drought-tolerant with few pests or diseases. Sow direct in spring (and autumn for winter crops). Protect seedlings from slugs, but once mature needs little attention.

Chicory
High-yielding and drought-tolerant with few pests or diseases. Sow in midsummer, sprinkling seeds direct along pre-watered drills. Thin to 15cm (6in) apart or grow as baby leaves for winter salads.

Chapter 2

Where to Grow

How much space do I need to be self-sufficient?

EVERYONE CAN GROW A LITTLE OF THEIR OWN FOOD, **even if it's just a few potted herbs on the windowsill. But what if you want to do more? How big a garden do you need to provide all your home-grown veg?**

It's perfectly feasible to be self-sufficient in all the fresh fruit, herbs and vegetables you need from an allotment-sized veg patch. The key is military-level organization. Plan your growing year in meticulous detail, working out exactly how much to provide at what times of the year and using every bit of your veg plot to the max, refilling beds repeatedly with new crops as they empty.

Then work out what you need to sow when, adding a little extra to allow for setbacks. If all goes well, you should be able to grow a wide enough variety, in enough quantity, to avoid the fresh produce aisle in your supermarket all year.

The standard measurement for an allotment is 10 rods – about 250sq m (2,690sq ft) – and this is based on the amount of land needed to feed a family of four. But even if your garden is smaller, you can still be self-sufficient in many kinds of fresh food.

Small-scale self-sufficiency

Even in small gardens, though, you can still be self-sufficient in a long list of foods. In fact, all you need is space for three roomy pots for year-round supplies of baby-leaf salads, plus fast-growing roots like round-rooted carrots and beetroot.

There's no reason you should ever have to buy spinach from the shops if you grow chard: sow in spring and

◀ If you have a little more space, you could utilize three raised beds as three-pot veg plots (see opposite) on a larger scale.

THREE-POT VEG PLOTS

All you need for year-round baby-leaf salads is three large containers.

- Sow each pot with baby-leaf salad mix, one month apart.

- When you've sown the last pot, start picking from the first.

- Once plants are spent, clear and resow.

- Repeat all year round, switching to winter varieties from late summer.

▲ The three-pot method also works for other fast-growing veg: try round-rooted carrots, salad turnips (above) and beetroot.

again in late summer to pick all year round. You can have kale somewhere on the plot all year, too: try different varieties or grow as baby leaves through summer. Pots of evergreen rosemary, thyme and bay mean you can tick fresh herbs off the shopping list, too.

Seasonal highlights

Other veg are more seasonal: but being self-sufficient doesn't mean having exactly the same vegetables on offer every day; just enough of whatever's available to feed yourself with.

There's a joy in letting your veg patch dictate what's on your plate, and eating seasonally makes food exciting again, too. When you've waited for each new treat, from succulent asparagus spears or sweet strawberries, every meal becomes a celebration!

Bay, *Laurus nobilis*

Rosemary, *Salvia rosmarinus*

What qualities should I look for in a good veg garden?

WHEN STARTING A NEW VEG PLOT you want it to be the best it can be. But whether you're picking a spot in your current garden or choosing an allotment plot, what should you look for to boost your chances of success?

South- or southwest-facing sites are sunniest, though a little shade is fine for lettuces, parsley and spinach.

A gentle slope isn't a problem, but steep slopes require terracing to work well. Good soil is not essential as you can improve the quality yourself: find out what soil you have as a starting point (see right). You can also beat back perennial weeds over time. Install rainwater harvesting and build a tool shed from reclaimed wood – and your new veg garden is good to go!

Parsley
Petroselinum crispum

The ideal spot for growing veg is sunny, sheltered and flat, with deep, rich soil. It has a good supply of water and it's close to your kitchen. Oh... and no perennial weeds! In practice, few veg patches are that perfect. As long as your would-be plot has sunshine, is reasonably flat and fairly sheltered, the rest you can work on.

HOW TO TEST SOIL

Most soils are a blend of materials. To find out which is dominant in your garden, take a fistful of soil and squeeze it.

Clay soil holds together easily. It's nutritious, but gets waterlogged. Avoiding digging helps (see page 128).

Sandy soil won't form a ball: it's easy to work all year round, but dries out quickly. Mulch often.

Chalky soil doesn't hold together and is greyish and stony. It's easy to work but thin, so improve with mulch.

What food can I grow in a shady courtyard?

Veg patches usually occupy the sunniest spot in the garden to boost flowers and fruit and guarantee great harvests. But what if there are no sunny spots – is there any food that grows well in a shady garden?

Every vegetable garden needs a few shady spots, especially for leafy vegetables and salads which tend to bolt and turn bitter in full sun. Many other veg, fruit and herbs grow well in shade too, so your garden could be well-stocked even without day-long sunshine.

Really, the only crops that must have sun are those which flower and fruit. Tomatoes, most beans (broad beans tolerate some shade), peas and courgettes won't produce good crops without lots of sunshine.

But if you eat leaves or roots rather than fruits, shade is less of a problem. Partial shade (two to six hours of sunshine a day) is all you need to grow root veg, brassicas, leafy veg and salads, plus a range of shade-loving herbs. Berry fruit and alpine strawberries also fruit fairly well in shade.

If the shade comes from mature trees, the poor, dry soil beneath will cause more problems than the lack of light: move your veg to the edge of the canopy if you can, and plant in raised beds where they won't have as much competition from tree roots.

TEN OF THE BEST FOODS FOR SHADY GARDENS

- Lettuce
- Kale
- Spinach
- Beetroot
- Chervil
- Parsley
- Mint
- Rhubarb
- Alpine strawberries
- Blackcurrants

Spinach,
Spinacia oleracea

Q I can't bend down much – what can I grow?

GARDENING CAN BE QUITE PHYSICALLY DEMANDING – hoeing, planting, weeding, let alone hauling compost bags about or moving planted-up containers. But what if you can't bend down or have arthritis, so struggle to hold hand tools? Can you still keep growing your own veg?

If you can't bend down to your veg, bring them up to you! Raised beds, elevated or 'tabletop' gardens – 30–45cm (12–18in)-deep planters on legs – and tall, wide containers mean you can garden while sitting or standing.

Gauge heights carefully, as you should work slightly downwards – gardening with raised arms is tiring. If sitting, 60cm (24in) is a good height, but raise that to 75cm (30in) if standing. A maximum width of 1.2m (4ft) lets you reach into the centre from the side.

Fill tabletop gardens with a 50:50 mix of topsoil and organic matter, and mulch annually to top up the soil levels and keep moisture in.

ACCESSIBLE GARDENING TIPS

Seed-sowing help
Cut a length of 25mm (1in) plumbing pipe and use it to sow seeds without having to bend down: aim the pipe along the drill and feed seeds in as you go.

Handy access hooks
Install cup hooks beneath tabletop planters; these can be used to store tools where they're easy to access but out of the rain.

Add toe holes
Slice 10cm (4in) off the bottom of the lowest plank of raised beds to make a 'toe hole' to slip your feet into so you don't have to bend forwards to work.

USEFUL WEBSITES

Thrive (carryongardening.org.uk) offers detailed advice for gardeners with specific issues, from strokes and sight loss to mobility problems.

Versus Arthritis (versusarthritis.org) has a free 'Gardening and Arthritis' booklet to download.

Disabled Living Foundation (livingmadeeasy.org.uk) lists ergonomic gardening tools and where to buy them.

The Gardening with Disabilities Trust (gardeningwithdisabilitiestrust. org.uk) gives grants to help gardeners adapt their growing spaces to make gardening easier.

Best crops to grow

Stick to shallow-rooted veg, such as salads, leafy veg, bush tomatoes and herbs, for tabletop gardens. Try patio varieties like the courgette 'Patio Star' or 'Hestia' runner beans.

In conventional raised beds, it's wise to choose low-growing veg – dwarf French beans rather than climbing varieties – and short-rooted crops like carrots, beetroot or onions, so you don't have to dig deeply to harvest. Add fruit with strawberries, dwarf varieties of raspberries – like 'Ruby Beauty' – and miniature apple, pear or plum trees grafted onto ultra-dwarfing rootstocks.

Buy tools that make gardening easier – for example, forks and spades with extendable handles – plus a sturdy trolley for easy transportation. Wear

You don't have to stop gardening just because you have mobility issues. In fact, it's often important you don't. Gentle exercise keeps you moving and boosts mental health, too. Design your garden carefully, make the most of specialist tools and plant well-behaved veg which are less demanding to grow, so gardening can be as much a part of your life as ever.

gloves and boots and change your position regularly to keep yourself comfortable so that, hopefully, you can stay and work in your garden until the sun goes down.

Do I need to rotate my crops?

VEG GROWERS ARE OFTEN TOLD not to grow crops in the same place year after year and to rotate them around the plot to avoid pests and diseases building up. Does it really make that much difference?

To follow a classic crop rotation, divide your garden into four areas. Plant one 'family' of crops in each area: the four families are potatoes; legumes (peas and beans); brassicas (cabbages, sprouts, broccoli and the like); and roots (including onions, garlic, leeks and shallots).

Each family group uses similar nutrients in the soil and suffers from the same pests and diseases (cabbage root fly, for example, attacks all brassicas, but won't affect potatoes). Move each family into a different bed each year and they start each season in fresh soil that's clean of pests.

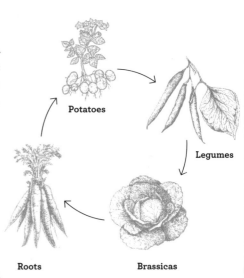

Potatoes

Legumes

Roots

Brassicas

▲ Each 'family' of vegetables can benefit the next – so nitrogen-fixing legumes help enrich the soil for big, greedy brassicas.

Crop rotation was invented by farmers to avoid the soil becoming 'sick' (depleted of nutrients) following year after year of the same crop. It's a good principle to follow if you can, but in small gardens it's difficult to move crops far enough to make it effective – and there are other ways to achieve similar results.

A more relaxed approach?

But do you need to be so strict? Return the full range of organic nutrients to the soil with mulches and no bed should get 'sick'. Moving carrots down the garden won't stop carrot fly zeroing in on their scent and diseases carried by rain or wind infect your crops wherever they're growing.

TRADITIONAL ROTATION PLAN

Plan your rotation so there's a gap of at least three years before planting the same crop in each space again to leave enough time for the soil nutrients to replenish and pests to die out.

	Year 1	Year 2	Year 3	Year 4
Bed 1	Potatoes	Legumes	Brassicas	Roots
Bed 2	Roots	Potatoes	Legumes	Brassicas
Bed 3	Brassicas	Roots	Potatoes	Legumes
Bed 4	Legumes	Brassicas	Roots	Potatoes

- On acidic soil, spread wood ash or garden lime after legumes are out for lime-loving brassicas.

- Add lashings of manure after lifting onions and roots to create rich soil for potatoes.

- Cut top growth away but leave roots to rot naturally and return nitrogen to the soil.

- 'Go anywhere' crops include squash, beetroot, spinach, lettuce and sweetcorn – you can pop them in wherever you have space.

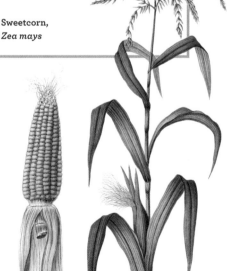

Sweetcorn,
Zea mays

The exceptions are fungal diseases lurking in the soil. Clubroot, verticillium wilt, fusarium wilt and onion white rot can all reinfect crops for years (see page 185). Rotation helps avoid the buildup of fungal diseases, but once you have them, they outlive a four-year rotation – so grow resistant varieties instead.

Can I grow potatoes in pots?

WHEN YOUR GARDEN IS
ON THE BIJOU SIDE OF
SMALL – or you don't have a
garden at all – it's a squeeze to
fit in any vegetables, let alone
space-hoggers like potatoes.
One solution is to grow them in
containers. But can potatoes
grow in pots?

It's always worth growing your
own potatoes: you'll know
they're free from pesticides
and they taste wonderful when
harvested fresh. But they do
take up lots of room, so
growing in pots and sacks is a
great solution for shoehorning
spuds into smaller spaces.
You'll get lower yields, but
containers let you grow out of
season – so it's worth trying
even in larger gardens.

FIVE POTATOES TO GROW IN POTS

'**Lady Christl**' Scored highest
for yield in container-grown
RHS trials.

'**Maris Peer**' Fine traditional
first early with a rich flavour.

'**Jazzy**' Waxy with a sweet,
'new potato' flavour.

'**Casablanca**' Large numbers of
waxy, white-skinned tubers.

'**Accord**' Creamy white and
tasty tubers.

Half-fill large, 40–50 litre (9–11
gallon) sacks (old compost sacks
work well) or 45cm (1½ft) diameter
containers with potting compost, either
home-made (see page 156) or peat-free
multipurpose. Add two handfuls
(125g/4oz) of organic potato fertilizer.

Plant five seed potatoes in the
compost, sprouted (or 'chitted') for a
few weeks before planting to enable
them to grow more quickly. As they
grow, add more compost to cover the
stems until the sack is full. Water daily,
adding comfrey feed (see page 124) or
liquid seaweed feed to the watering can

BUILD A POTATO BOX

Potato boxes are high-rise living for spuds: they take up just 60cm (2ft) square – enough for five seed potatoes – and they're built straight onto soil, so give higher yields than containers.

1 Screw the first layer of planks, 60cm (2ft) long, to four 1m (3ft)-tall upright posts to start making a box.

2 Add a second layer of planks, then half-fill with garden compost and topsoil, mixed at 50:50.

3 Put seed potatoes on top, then cover with more compost mix.

4 Screw on additional layers of planks, filling with compost mix to earth up stems as they grow.

5 To harvest, simply take the front off the box and collect your spuds: you can use the same box again next year.

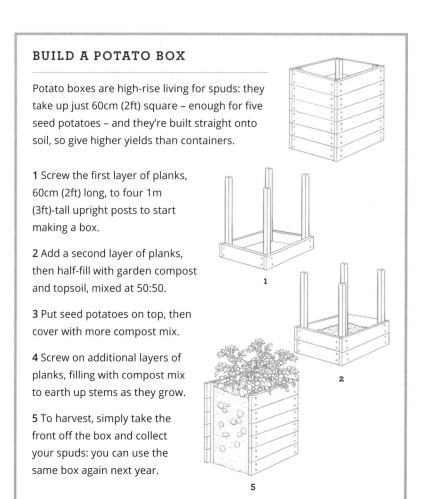

weekly. When the plants start flowering, they're ready: gently rummage down and extract the largest, leaving the rest to grow or just tip the lot out at once.

The benefits of containers

You'll get a lower yield when you grow in containers – about half what you'd get in the ground. The best returns are from first earlies ('new' potatoes), which are smaller and grow more quickly. Pots and sacks make up for their modest harvests by being portable, so you can plant much earlier than garden-grown. Start seed potatoes in sacks as early as late winter indoors, move them outside after the last frost and you'll be eating new potatoes by late spring – months earlier than if you'd grown them in the open garden.

Q Can I grow veg on my compost heap?

COMPOST HEAPS ARE CONCENTRATED PILES OF GOODNESS, a melting pot of nutrients, minerals and trace elements released as kitchen scraps, lawn clippings and old plants rot down. So does that make them good places to grow vegetables?

Planting into compost heaps is good for both plants and compost: roots relish the moist, nutrient-rich environment and – as they grow – they aerate your compost. And let's face it, compost bins aren't pretty, so covering them with a riot of pumpkins and nasturtiums is a big improvement.

Compost bins are rough-and-tumble places and pure compost (even well-rotted) can be too rich for very young plants, so don't sow straight into the top. Raise plants under cover until they fill a 10cm (4in) pot, then make a hollow in the heap, fill with potting compost and plant into that.

A Well-rotted compost is sheer heaven for plants, especially big, greedy ones like pumpkins, squash and tomatoes. In fact, many sustainable gardening techniques harness the power of the heap to supercharge growth without artificial fertilizers, giving superb results just by collecting and recycling organic waste.

▼ Make sure you choose a heap you don't need any compost from for now – once planted, you won't be able to disturb it.

COMPOST HEAP GARDENING

Hotbeds

Trap the heat given off by fresh manure as it rots and you have a mini heated greenhouse. Dig a hole or build an above-ground box at least 60cm (2ft) square and fill with manure. Monitor the temperature; once it falls to 20°C (68°F), top up with compost and plant.

△ Cover hotbeds with cloches to bring on super-early crops in spring.

Keyhole beds

All compost heaps leach nutrient-rich liquid – so if you grow veg alongside, they're fed automatically. Make a central compost bin from chicken wire, then construct a raised bed around it (make a channel to access the bin). Water through the bin's contents to feed your plants.

Lasagne gardens

Build a compost heap on the ground in autumn and by spring it'll be a nutritious veg bed ready to plant. Start with a layer of dampened newspaper followed by layers of organic matter like straw, grass clippings or autumn leaves. Top with compost and plant in spring (see page 131 for more details).

Maximize your heap

Plants that enjoy compost bins tend to be big characters like pumpkins, winter squash, courgettes and runner beans. Avoid potatoes, as the baby tubers they leave behind in the compost resprout when you come to use it.

You don't have to stick to bins, either: bespoke compost heaps can turbo-charge your growing anywhere in the veg garden. Hotboxes, keyhole beds and lasagne gardens (see above) exploit the high nutrient levels and warmth given off by rotting organic matter to bring on early veg in spring, create rich gardens on poor soil and make new veg beds with minimum effort. Not a bad result from a load of garden rubbish!

Do grow lights make seedlings grow better?

SEEDLINGS NEED BOTH WARMTH AND LIGHT to succeed. You can provide warmth with a heated propagator, but extending daylight is trickier – especially in the short, dark days of early spring. Can grow lights help early-sown seedlings grow better?

Light levels are surprisingly low indoors, even near a window: you've probably noticed windowsill seedlings grow leggy and weak as they stretch towards sunlight. Although domestic lightbulbs seem bright to us, their light isn't intense enough for plants to thrive.

Grow lights, however, are designed to give out exactly the light wavelengths seedlings need to grow upright, stocky and healthy, just as they would in natural daylight. They're now readily available to home gardeners, inexpensive and easy to use.

▲ Short, stocky seedlings turn into healthier plants with stronger, straighter stems when germinated under grow lights.

Many crops – including tomatoes, aubergines and peppers – need sowing early to give them a long enough growing season. But out-of-season light levels are so gloomy, the resulting seedlings are often weak and spindly. Grow lights mimic the light spectrum of natural sunshine, so your seedlings can bask as if it's the height of spring.

HOW PLANTS USE LIGHT

Plants 'eat' light, absorbing it and converting it via photosynthesis into the energy they need to grow. But the light they use isn't the light we humans see. We notice yellow and white light – whereas plants 'see' everything in red, blue and ultraviolet, a wavelength completely invisible to us.

Red light is dominant in summer and autumn; it prompts lots of tall, fast growth and flowering, and governs seed germination too. Blue light is plentiful in spring: it triggers plant growth and development but keeps plants shorter (so seedlings grow sturdier). In practice, plants need a mix of both all year round in order to grow and develop healthily.

LED grow lights

LED (light emitting diode) grow lights are more expensive than traditional fluorescent tubes but they're more energy efficient and last longer. Full-spectrum white LED grow lights are good all-round choices, but if you want specialist lights for seedlings, go for blue spectrum (sometimes referred to as 6,500k) lights rather than red (2,700k) which stimulate flowering.

Hang LED lights 15–30cm (6–12in) above seedling trays and add a timer, set to turn the lights on for about 16 hours a day – no longer, as plants need a nighttime rest too. Grow lights aren't just for spring seedlings, either: hang them over trays of baby-leaf lettuce seedlings and you can raise year-round crops of indoor salads as well.

◀ Look at the leaves to check the plant is getting the right light levels. Bleached or yellowish leaves are getting too much light; but if they've turned dark green, turn up the brightness.

Do I need to use plastic pots and trays to grow my veg?

BRITISH GARDENERS GET THROUGH about 500 million new plastic plant pots and modules every year. Less than half are recycled; the rest end up incinerated, in landfill or polluting the oceans. But is plastic really necessary for growing veg?

Wooden seedtrays make an easy like-for-like replacement for plastic. They can be expensive to buy, but you can make them yourself from scrap wood. Line with newspaper before filling with compost, then sow exactly as for plastic. Wood is porous, so dries out quicker, but seedlings seem to relish the extra air and water flow, and so thrive in wooden trays.

For sowing into modules and pricking out seedlings, newspaper pots are ideal. These are quick to make using a paper potter or straight-sided shot glass. Other plastic-free sowing

FIVE-POINT PLAN FOR REDUCING PLASTIC IN THE GARDEN

1 Buy no new plastic – including pots with new plants; instead, buy bare-root or raise from seeds or cuttings.

2 Use up the plastic you have.

3 Recycle spent plastic.

4 Find biodegradable alternatives, from hessian grow bags to metal watering cans.

5 If there's no non-plastic alternative, find another way.

🔽 Keep the diameter of newspaper pots small – no more than around 5cm (2in) – so they stay rigid and can withstand watering.

options include cardboard toilet roll inners for larger seeds and soil blocks made from compressed compost.

Easy potting on

Pot module-grown seedlings on, just as they are, into pulp pots (which you will have to buy in) or cardboard pots (made at home for free). In biodegradable pots, roots grow straight through the sides without circling as they do in plastic, so pot-bound plants become a thing of the past. You plant the whole thing, without removing the pot first – don't worry if the cardboard has already started to degrade, the plant doesn't mind. Roots unconstrained by plastic shoot straight out into the soil, so your plant can get growing straightaway, just as nature intended.

Plastic has only been widely used in gardening for about 50 years – and gardeners have grown veg very successfully for much longer than that! In fact, there's some evidence seedlings grow better in wooden seedtrays and that plants establish more quickly in biodegradable pots – so switching away from plastic could even improve results.

Vipots, made from grain hulls, make good lightweight alternatives to new clay pots. Better still are fibre pots and modules, buried with the plant to biodegrade naturally in the soil.

HOW TO MAKE A CARDBOARD POT

You will need
• Thin, plain cardboard
• Pencil
• Ruler
• Scissors
• Paper masking tape

1 Draw a template for an open-top box, whatever size you want.

2 Cut it out, then score along the folds around the central square.

3 Fold the sides up to meet each other and tape together with masking tape.

2

4 Fill with compost and plant up.

Can strawberries grow in shade?

YOU LOVE STRAWBERRIES – but your veg patch is overshadowed by a tree or a neighbouring building. Does that mean you have to give up on your favourite sun-loving fruit?

All plants have preferences. Spinach likes cool shade, blueberries grow in damp, acidic soil, and strawberries fruit best in sunshine. Match your plants to the conditions they like and they'll perform to their full potential, giving you the bumper harvests you want.

If you don't have the right conditions in your garden to grow the plants you'd like, just think laterally.

It's important to grow plants in the place that suits them best – and large-fruited dessert strawberries are all about summer sunshine. But there are over 100 different species of strawberry and hundreds more varieties – including many that thrive in shade. Plant one of those instead and you can pick all the sweet treats you want.

HOW TO GROW ALPINE STRAWBERRIES

Alpine varieties, also known as wild strawberries, are among the easiest to grow. Simply sow from seed in spring, then plant out 20–30cm (8–12in) apart in partial shade, either in containers, hanging baskets or the garden. After that they need very little care, growing steadily into a mat of dense ground cover spangled with flowers and fruits all summer.

FIVE OF THE BEST ALPINE STRAWBERRIES

'Alexandria' Fruits particularly well in shade, with dozens of small, sweet strawberries.

'Mara des Bois' The best flavour of all the alpines, with larger fruit.

'Baron von Solemacher' Abundant clusters of sweet, aromatic fruit.

'Mignonette' Compact French heirloom with masses of tiny fruit; good in hanging baskets.

'Yellow Wonder' Pale yellow fruit with an intense, pineappley flavour.

Alpine strawberry,
Fragaria vesca

Match plants to your patch

Malabar spinach is a sun-loving climber with lush, plentiful leaves – it's a great substitute for traditional spinach, which tends to bolt in hot weather. If your soil is alkaline, grow blueberries in containers of peat-free ericaceous (acidic) compost. And pack shady fruit gardens with morello cherries and blackcurrants, which don't need much sun to fruit well.

Strawberries for shade

The big, fat dessert strawberries you find at Wimbledon (*Fragaria* × *ananassa*) produce some fruit in dappled shade but a fraction of what you'd get in sun. Alpine strawberries (*Fragaria vesca*), on the other hand, actively prefer a little shade.

The fruits are small but intensely flavoured, and they'll carry on right up to the first frosts. The true wild strawberry has really tiny fruits, but there are larger-fruited varieties, giving you plenty to pick over a longer period of time than you'd get with dessert strawberries – and many would argue with a better flavour, too!

Can I grow a whole veg garden in a container?

MOST GARDENERS GROW AT LEAST SOME **vegetables in containers. But rather than restricting yourself to one variety of vegetable per pot, what if you mix it up? Can you turn a container into a potted veg plot?**

Plant your one-pot veg plot in a big container: 45cm (18in) in diameter is a minimum, but go larger if you can. Terracotta is traditional (buying secondhand has a lower carbon footprint), but you can also repurpose tin baths and water troughs, or build wooden planters from reclaimed scaffold boards.

Fill your container with some home-made potting compost (see page 156) or peat-free multipurpose compost – ideally a soil-based one (look for 'John Innes' on the bag). Mix in a couple of handfuls of seaweed meal, then get planting!

Sowing and planting

Sow most veg separately, under cover, and plant into the container as young plants. Root crops – such as carrots, turnips and beetroot – and annual herbs, like coriander, can be sown direct. Choose compact patio varieties wherever possible, as they're bred to thrive in pots; there are dwarf varieties of most types of veg now, from Brussels sprouts ('Half Tall') to runner beans ('Hestia'). Long-cropping, 'cut-and-come-again' veg like loose-leaf lettuces and chard are invaluable as they let you pick for weeks without replanting.

Put the tallest plants in first, with supports if required; then surround them with mid-size plants, spaced 10–15cm (4–6in) apart. Finally, add

After harvesting fast-growing crops, fill the gaps with a little fresh compost, replanting with pre-sown young plants to enable picking until the first frosts.

CONTAINER VEG RECIPES

Sunday roast veg
- Mangetout pea 'Shiraz'
- Carrot 'Parmex'
- Beetroot 'Boltardy'
- Parsley 'Moss Green Curled'

Salads galore
- Cucumber 'Patio Snacker'
- Lettuce 'Salad Bowl'
- Radish 'Sparkler'
- Chervil
- Corn salad

Cucumber,
Cucumis sativus

Pasta sauce pot
- Tomato 'Mountain Magic'
- Basil 'Genovese'
- Spring onion 'White Lisbon'
- Marjoram

Eat your greens
- Kale 'Red Russian'
- Calabrese 'Kabuki'
- Chard
- New Zealand spinach

Basil, *Ocimum basilicum*

low-growing herbs, strawberries or salad leaves around the edge to ensure enough light gets to every plant.

Group vegetables that enjoy similar growing conditions in the same pot, then have fun trying different combinations. You could grow all the veg you'd use in your favourite recipe or go for a mixed salad with leaves, herbs and larger ingredients such as tomatoes, cucumbers or radishes to feast on all summer long.

Think of veg plot containers as bedding combinations you can eat. Combine thrillers (taller plants such as beans or peas), fillers (mid-sized plants like chard) and low-growing spillers to froth over the edges for a veg plot that looks as good as it tastes.

Do I need soil to grow my own food?

INDOOR GARDENING AND COMPOST aren't always happy partners: if you've ever tried potting up lettuces in the kitchen, you'll know what a mess it makes. But can you ditch the compost and still grow food?

There are two types of hydroponic systems: nutrient film – with plant roots suspended in nutrient-rich water – and substrate systems in which plants are rooted into coir or rockwool, then immersed.

Either system gives you blemish-free, pesticide-free crops, about a third of the time quicker than soil-grown methods. Organic nutrient mixes are more eco-friendly, although plants grow a little slower. Use LED grow lights (see page 73) and you'll be able to grow your own all year round. Another benefit is that you never have to remember to do the watering.

Hydroponic growing has an environmental cost: artificial fertilizers, coir or rockwool substrates and plastic accessories all add to this.

Soilless growing (known as hydroponics) is revolutionizing veg growing. It has made it possible to grow salads, kale, tomatoes and strawberries in the most unlikely of places, from underground subway tunnels to the International Space Station. You can use the same technology at home.

Build a hydroponic system

You could buy a ready-made hydroponics kit – or make your own.

Start by sowing your veg onto coir starter discs. Then fill a container with water and add nutrient mix (from hydroponics suppliers). Add a fish tank pump and grow lights. Then fit a polystyrene lid with holes cut in, slot in aquatic pots with a plant in each and watch them grow! Keep the system's pH at about 6.0, monitoring it with test papers. Add some citric acid to lower the pH or baking soda to raise it.

Is it a good idea to grow food in my front garden?

IF YOU'RE LOOKING FOR THE VEG PATCH, it's probably in the back garden where it's more private. But what if your front garden is sunnier or the only growing space you have?

Growing vegetables in the front garden might not be traditional – but sometimes it's your only option. Once filled with mouth-watering produce it'll become a real talking point – who knows, you might inspire the neighbours to do the same!

A front garden bursting with fruit and veg provides a lovely welcome. It's also good for you and your neighbours: plants in front gardens improve air quality, reduce stress levels and absorb excess rainwater, so your street doesn't flood.

In cities, a roadside hedge shields crops from air-borne pollution. Test soil for contaminants before planting, or grow in containers instead. Check local bylaws, as there are extra rules governing front gardens, and if you rent, ask your landlord's permission.

FRONT GARDEN DESIGN TIPS

Make a potager with a simple geometric pattern picked out in low clipped hedges.

Plant pretty vegetables like scarlet ruby chard (below), slate-blue 'Bleu de Solaise' leeks and purple 'Shiraz' mangetout peas.

Use walls for climbing beans, tomatoes and cucumbers to scramble up.

Can I grow fruit trees in pots?

YOU MAY NOT HAVE SPACE for a spreading orchard of apple, plum and pear trees, but there's still room for fruit – plant a potted orchard instead. But can you really grow fruit trees in pots?

Fruit trees grafted onto dwarfing rootstocks grow just 2m (6½ft) tall, small enough to cope with life in a roomy pot. And for some fruit, there are positive advantages to growing in containers. Fruit in pots needs careful watering and feeding, but should give you plenty to fill your fruit bowl for many years.

The secret behind pot-sized fruit trees is the rootstock. This governs the size of the eventual tree, and dwarfing rootstocks produce tiny trees – ideal for containers.

Look on the label or ask your supplier to check you have the right one. For apples, M9 or M26 are good choices; pears should be grafted onto Quince C, cherries on Colt or Gisela 5, and plums and peaches on Pixy or

FRUIT TREES DESIGNED FOR PATIO GROWING

Quince 'Sibley's Patio Quince'

Cherry 'Porthos'

Mulberry 'Matsunaga'

Fig 'Brown Turkey'

Apricot 'Flavorcot'

 Citrus trees grow happily in pots – and they're much easier to move in under cover for winter, keeping them frost-free until spring.

CARING FOR POTTED ORCHARDS

Water potted fruit trees twice weekly – daily in dry weather – letting the compost dry a little between waterings.

Add high-potassium comfrey, seaweed or tomato feed to the watering can fortnightly.

Mulch with home-made compost or leafmould each spring.

Repot into a larger pot every 2–3 years, or prune the roots: gently tip the tree out of its pot and cut away about a quarter of the roots, then return to the pot with fresh compost.

In winter, raise pots off the ground on pot feet to drain off excess rainwater, and wrap containers in straw and hessian to prevent roots freezing.

Fig, *Ficus carica*

Best fruit trees for pots

Fig trees fruit better when their roots are confined and citrus trees grown in pots are much easier to move under cover for winter. Potted peaches and apricots are also more easily sheltered from rain, avoiding the rain-borne fungal disease peach leaf curl.

Planting your trees

Plant fruit trees into large, wide-based, heavy pots at least 60cm (2ft) across and deep, using a mix of three parts garden topsoil, three parts loam-based, peat-free compost and one part grit, with a couple of handfuls of seaweed meal mixed in. Water the tree in well and your patio orchard is ready to enjoy and savour!

St Julien A. Or just choose a Minarette® tree: these are vertical cordons, trained to grow upright on a single stem and kept that way by annual pruning. Remember too that self-fertile fruit varieties don't require a partner, so you only need one tree for a good crop.

Q Can I grow carrots in my kitchen?

INSIDE YOUR HOME THERE'S A MINI ALLOTMENT plot just waiting to be used. Windowsills offer light, warmth and convenience – but what can you grow there? Can you grow carrots in your kitchen?

A Windowsill farms are surprisingly productive, pumping out salad leaves, plus herbs and extras like chilli peppers. Even carrots are possible on windowsills (as long as you choose baby round-rooted 'Paris Market' types), but you won't fit many in a pot, so it's more satisfying to sprout the tops for their edible foliage instead.

Sprouting kitchen scraps is a great project to try with the kids as it doesn't need any special equipment: just cut the tops off some carrots and pop onto a saucer lined with soaked cotton wool or kitchen towel. Tufts of ferny foliage appear within a few days: once they're 15cm (6in) tall, snip them away to make carrot top pesto or pan-fry with olive oil and garlic. You can also try this with turnips and beetroot (for scrummy, burgundy-tinged salad leaves).

MICROGREEN FARMING

Microgreens are vegetables eaten as intensely flavoured seedlings and are incredibly quick to grow – you'll be harvesting the fastest within ten days. Radish, beetroot, broccoli and pea shoots are all delicious, although you can try any type of vegetable except parsnips (which are poisonous at seedling stage). Lay 2–3cm ($3/4$–1in) of potting compost in a tray and sow generously, then cover with more compost and keep watered. Snip seedlings at 7–10cm (3–4in) tall.

Radish (*Raphanus sativus*) sprouts

THREE EDIBLE HOUSEPLANTS

Chillies
Choose your brightest
windowsill and grow
compact varieties such as
fiery 'Zimbabwe Bird' or
perhaps multicoloured
'Numex Twilight'.

Lemongrass
Citrusy Thai spice that
happily doubles as a
houseplant: root stems
from the shops in water,
then pot up in compost.

Ginger
Half-bury an organic rhizome
from the supermarket in
potting compost, keep warm
and it will grow into a tall,
bamboo-like houseplant:
harvest stems and roots.

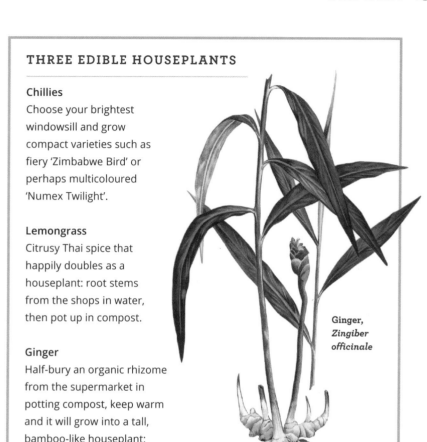

Ginger,
*Zingiber
officinale*

Windowsill herbs

You don't have to stop with carrot,
beetroot and parsnip tops (see
opposite). Pot up summer herbs like
mint and marjoram from the garden to
grow on the kitchen windowsill in
autumn and they stay green well into
winter. Sow parsley, coriander and
Greek basil in windowsill pots and
trays for fragrant annual herbs.

Windowsill salads

Windowsill farms come into their own
for growing mouth-watering gourmet
salads. Sow baby-leaf lettuces, spinach
and kale, pea shoots and microgreens
in trays of potting compost every few
weeks for a continuous supply,
replacing each tray as soon as it's
harvested, and you can feast all year
without leaving your front door.

Q What can I grow on the roof of my shed?

WHEN SPACE IS AT A PREMIUM, every planting opportunity counts. So don't just stay on the ground – head skywards! Shed roofs are lovely open areas begging to be planted, so what veg can you grow up there?

Before you start, make sure your shed is suitable for a green roof. Wet compost plus plants can be really heavy, so you'll need a well-built shed, with a gently sloping roof – ideally no steeper than a 20-degree angle. If you're worried, build the green roof on an external frame which holds it up independent of the shed itself.

Build the roof in layers, starting with a waterproof membrane of reclaimed pond liner or heavy-duty plastic to protect the roof itself. Staple this over the shed roof, then build a frame for the planting bed on top, using 15cm (6in)-wide wooden planks screwed firmly onto the shed sides to make a raised box. Drill drainage holes

2cm (3/4in) wide at the lower end and add blocks in each corner, screwing the planks to them to lock the whole thing together. Build a ladder, or even better some steps, into your supporting frame, so you can get up on to the roof easily for weeding, watering and, of course, harvesting!

Preparing to plant

Add a 2cm (3/4in) layer of gravel, followed by a layer of weed-proof membrane (garden felt is a plastic-free but shorter-lived alternative) stapled firmly to the frame. Finally, fill with a 3:1 mix of peat-free multipurpose compost and lightweight drainage material: dried rice husks or crushed

Build a tabletop planter on top of your bike shed or bin store and fill to overflowing with herbs and strawberries.

The top of your shed is not a place for lettuce leaves, as they'll dry out too quickly. Instead, plant robust Mediterranean herbs (like rosemary, sage and thyme), alpine strawberries and low-growing edible flowers for fragrance, flavour and brilliant colour all summer long.

Creeping thyme,
Thymus serpyllum

shells are more eco-friendly alternatives to high-carbon hydroleca or perlite. And that's it – your rooftop veg patch is ready to plant!

Other rooftop possibilities

Don't stop at the shed: green bin stores, bike sheds and even the guinea pig hutch are potential rooftop veg patches. They're often more sheltered, so you can expand into salads and leafy greens.

Common violet,
Viola odorata

LOOKING AFTER YOUR GREEN ROOF

Your green roof will need the most attention in the first year after planting. Water daily in hot weather, paying particular attention to plants near the apex where it dries out fastest. Remove any weed seedlings and feed with liquid seaweed once a fortnight. Replace any plants that fail and after 12–18 months your green roof should have knitted together to create a fragrant and edible carpet needing just an occasional tidy-up in return for transforming your shed into an oasis of greenery.

Can I use my hedges and fences for growing food?

ONCE YOU'RE USING EVERY INCH OF SPACE ON THE
GROUND, you've greened all your shed roofs and packed your
patio with pots – where next? How about fences and hedges
– can they help you grow more food?

Co-opt the vertical surfaces in
your garden and you double
the growing space. Add wires
or trellis to fences and walls to
grow climbing beans, squash,
maincrop peas, cucumbers and
trained fruit. Plant mixed
hedges full of fruit and berries
and they'll feed both you and
the local wildlife.

Pallets make great wall planters: nail
on extra wooden slats and line the back
with repurposed compost sacks to make
evenly spaced troughs.

Growing against walls and fences
means fruit and veg take up
hardly any space on the ground, so you
can plant other things around their
feet. You'll need sturdy supports such
as trellis or a system of vine eyes and
wires, with the first about 45cm (18in)
above ground and the rest in rows
spaced 15–30cm (6–12in) apart up the
wall or fence. Plant at the base, and tie
in as they grow.

Or just lift everything off the
ground and create a living wall. This is
ideal for courtyard gardens, alleyways
and balconies and can really boost
growth as walls act like heat pads,
creating a little microclimate around
your plants. Buy kits or make your own
by fixing planters firmly to a mesh

PLANTS FOR AN EDIBLE HEDGE

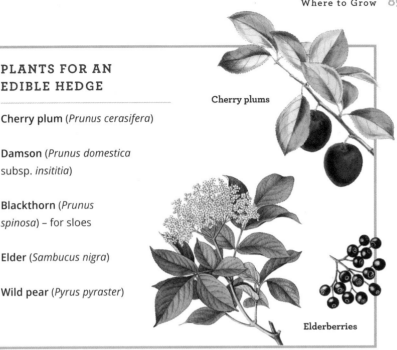

Cherry plums

Cherry plum (*Prunus cerasifera*)

Damson (*Prunus domestica* subsp. *insititia*)

Blackthorn (*Prunus spinosa*) – for sloes

Elder (*Sambucus nigra*)

Wild pear (*Pyrus pyraster*)

Elderberries

stapled to sturdy timber supports. 'Trough'-style planters work better than pockets as they allow roots to spread sideways. Plant sun-lovers like bush tomatoes and chillies at the top, graduating to leafy salads and shade-loving herbs at the base.

Gutter gardens are also great for growing leafy salads and herbs: fix lengths of deep guttering to a fence at 20–30cm (8–12in) intervals, add drainage holes and end stops (available from DIY stores), fill with compost and plant.

Edible hedges

Many of the plants you can clip into hedges also produce delicious berries or fruit, so plant an edible hedge and you have an ersatz orchard that doubles as your garden boundary. Edible hedges can be as simple as a row of closely planted (1m/3ft apart) blackcurrant, gooseberry or blueberry bushes useful for filtering the wind while providing tart fruit for jams and ice cream.

If you have plenty of space in your garden, you'll get the widest choice of fruit from an informal, natural-looking and wildlife-friendly mixed hedge. Plant bare-root saplings in winter, mixing at least four different species randomly through the hedge. Plant in staggered double rows, with each plant 30cm (1ft) apart, water and then mulch. Once your hedge reaches the height you want, start clipping annually in winter: you can expect fruit after two to three years.

How much veg can I grow on my balcony?

LOOK UP IN ANY CITY and you'll see bursts of greenery erupting from apartment blocks where balconies have been co-opted as gardens in the sky. So how much can you pick from a high-rise veg patch?

Clothe every surface of your balcony in edible greenery and you'll be surprised by how productive your sky garden can be.

A few large containers are better than lots of small ones as they don't dry out as easily. Major on patio veg, herbs and salads, especially cut-and-come-again veg like lettuces, chard and kale you can pick leaf by leaf for weeks. Heavy-cropping veg such as beans and cherry tomatoes also help you make the most of every inch of space.

CONSIDERATE BALCONY GARDENING

Check with your local council and landlord for any restrictions on planting your balcony – it is especially worth finding out the weight-bearing load, as pots filled with damp soil and plants are very heavy. Use lightweight containers made of materials such as tin, wood or wicker if you're unsure. Once your garden is up and running, keep the downstairs neighbours happy by using trays to catch excess water, so it doesn't drip over the edge.

Climbing beans curl happily around balconies, so you can use them as ersatz plant supports.

Maximize on growing space

To cloak the walls in greenery, plant a trough with tomatoes and French beans and train them upwards on trellises, or put up shelves lined with identical pots filled with alpine strawberries and chillies. Living walls and gutter gardens (see page 88) work well on balconies too.

Hang baskets dripping with cherry tomatoes from the ceiling and sling saddlebag planters over your railings, filling them with dwarf peas or mini cucumbers left without supports to trail downwards.

△ Fix trellis supports firmly to walls using screws and Rawlplugs® since tomatoes and climbing beans are heavy when fully laden.

Add ornamentals

Include flowers alongside the veg, not only to look pretty but also to attract passing insects who will pollinate your crops. And if you have room, make space for a little seat, so you can take time out to enjoy the oasis you've created in the sky.

Some balconies are just narrow strips, while others can accommodate a table and chairs: but all offer plenty of options for planting. As well as containers on the floor, you can plant up railings, walls and even ceilings to surround yourself with delicious things to harvest every day of the year.

BALCONY LIFE

Balconies are extreme places. At their best, they're microclimates surrounded by walls that act as storage heaters – a nirvana for plants. The flipside is that high-up gardens can be very exposed to weather.

Provide shelter from desiccating winds using reed screens attached to the railings; awnings help shade plants from parching sunshine too. Plants on balconies need regular watering, so drip irrigation or self-watering pots help keep the compost damp at all times.

Can I put a veg bed on my patio?

PATIOS ARE PRIME SPOTS FOR GROWING VEG: sunny, sheltered and close to the house. But they're also paved, so you can't plant into the ground. Apart from containers, what are your options – can you make veg beds on patios?

Beds allow you to grow vegetables almost as you would in the open garden; you'll harvest more than from containers. Create mini patio gardens by lifting paving slabs to expose the ground beneath, or simply build raised beds on top of slabs or gravel to harvest without leaving your sun lounger.

At its simplest, gardening a patio simply involves taking some of it up to access the earth beneath. Use a crowbar to lever up pavers in areas not needed for access or seating, then remove all the sand and hardcore until you reach bare soil. This will be dry and compacted, so break it up with a fork, then fill with a 50:50 mix of topsoil and home-made garden compost (see page 130) or soil improver and plant with herbs, or perhaps a patio courgette or some dwarf beans.

▶ Building your own raised bed means you can design it to fit your patio's dimensions exactly.

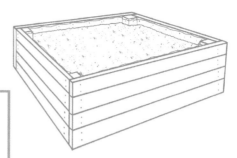

BUILDING RAISED BEDS ON CONCRETE

- Screw reclaimed wood to corner posts in two or three layers to make a box 30–60cm (1–2ft) high.

- Line the base with a layer of gravel or sharp sand 5–10cm (2–4in) deep.

- Cover with weed-suppressing fabric (garden felt is a plastic-free alternative, though may need replacing after a few years) and staple to the sides.

- Fill the bed with a 50:50 mix of topsoil and organic matter such as garden compost, green municipal waste or well-rotted farmyard manure.

- Water raised beds on concrete carefully to avoid any excess seeping out and staining the patio. If possible, site your raised bed at the edge of your patio, so water can drain into neighbouring soil. Hose off leakages promptly after watering.

If you can't lift slabs, or your patio is on solid concrete, just build a raised bed directly on top. Make a simple square or rectangle from reclaimed wood to sit directly on the hard standing, or build a long, deep planter, 60–90cm (2–3ft) wide, out of reclaimed wood – secondhand scaffold boards work brilliantly for this – to run along the patio's edge.

Which crops to grow?

Although patio gardens allow you to grow a much wider range of vegetables, room for roots is still restricted, so major on drought-tolerant veg such as chard, beetroot and cut-and-come-again lettuce. Terracing planters at different levels allows you to grow deep-rooted crops like carrots and parsnips in the tallest, with lower levels used for beans, tomatoes or cucumbers. Choose compact patio varieties that won't mind the limited conditions. Keep well-watered and feed regularly with home-made feed (see page 124) or liquid seaweed throughout the growing season.

Should I put a pond in my veg garden?

WHEN YOU HAVE A VEG GARDEN you want to put every square inch to work raising food. So why would you hand over good growing space to a pond?

▲ Birds love a pond, for drinking, bathing and snacking on the many insects it attracts.

Even if you can only spare enough room for a tiny washing-up bowl pond, it'll be a magnet for wildlife – and in a veg garden that means pest control. Frogs and toads hoover up slug eggs. Other visitors might include birds (for tackling aphids), bats (mosquitoes) and hedgehogs (caterpillars). Bees need to drink, too, so they're also regulars at ponds – pollinating your crops at the same time.

Formal straight-sided ponds, sunk in the ground or in above-ground tanks, are invaluable for collecting rainwater from nearby sheds, so you can dip in your watering can for speedy watering. Plant like any other pond, remembering to add an escape ramp for wildlife.

▼ Plant container and half-barrel ponds with miniature waterlilies and miniature bulrush (*Typha minima*).

Ponds were once commonplace in Victorian vegetable gardens, often right in the centre where gardeners could fill watering cans within easy reach of crops. Veg garden ponds attract wildlife (and therefore natural pest control), soften the effects of climate change and even provide food – all while looking lovely!

Benefits of a larger pond

Hand over up to 15 percent of your growing space to larger ponds and you open a whole new world of aquatic vegetables to try. Expanses of water reflect light onto your plants, and regulate temperatures, helping to smooth out extremes by absorbing

LOOKING AFTER YOUR VEG PATCH POND

Spring

- Sow seeds of aquatic crops like kangkong and watercress.

- Plant new aquatic plants or divide and replant existing ones.

- Harvest young emerging shoots and leaves.

Summer

- Top up ponds with rainwater in hot weather.

- Remove blanketweed by using a stick to twist it out.

- Cut kangkong and watercress leaves every few days.

Autumn

- Rake fallen leaves out of the pond to stop it silting up.

- Remove dead or dying leaves, so they don't rot into the water.

- Gather your harvest of tubers and rhizomes once foliage dies back.

Winter

- Melt ice with a pan of hot water to let oxygen through to creatures beneath.

- Remove and clean pond pumps and store until spring.

Watercress, *Nasturtium officinale*

Kangkong, *Ipomoea aquatica*

warmth, then releasing it slowly during cooler spells. They'll also absorb and slow some of the storm water from sudden downpours, so your veg garden is less likely to flood.

Greenhouse ponds

Install a small pond in the greenhouse and it'll absorb the sun's warmth all day, releasing it at night to keep your plants cosy and frost-free.

Do I have to remove the turf before I build my raised bed?

SO YOU'VE DECIDED TO TRANSFORM YOUR TATTY LAWN into a productive veg patch overflowing with good things to eat. But digging up turf is a backbreaking job – is there any other way to do it?

The traditional way to open up new veg beds was to clear the ground, strip away turf, then double dig the soil beneath. But that is unnecessary and does more harm than good. Build raised beds straight onto the grass – it's better for the environment, your veg and your back.

When you strip off turf, you're removing goodness from the ground: all that lush grass is full of nitrogen and helps feed your plants. Digging also ruins delicate subsoil ecosystems and exposes buried carbon to the air where it oxidizes into carbon dioxide.

Instead, set your lawnmower blades low and scalp the grass close to the ground. Then build your raised bed on top. Fill with a 50:50 mix of topsoil and soil improver – like garden compost, green municipal waste or well-rotted manure – and plant. It is as easy as that!

What about weeds?

Don't bother trying to dig out perennial weeds like bindweed, couch grass or ground elder: they'll resprout from the roots and grow straight back to infest your veg. Instead, cover the area with thick cardboard or garden felt before building your raised bed on top. This holds back perennial weeds for the best part of a season. Repeat as necessary, covering the bed with cardboard and deep mulch each spring, and you'll weaken them further until they eventually give up.

Can I use my pond to grow things to eat?

PONDS ARE WILDLIFE MAGNETS that fill your garden with darting, splashing life and provide endless fascination for the kids (and you). But can they double up as veg beds?

For rafts of nutritious greens to pick from your pond, grow kangkong (*Ipomoea aquatica*). It makes dense thickets of spinach-like leaves on bamboo-like stems, 30–40cm (12–16in) tall, and is delicious stir-fried with ginger and garlic. Or there's peppery watercress, best grown in barrel ponds

Kangkong, *Ipomoea aquatica*

beneath rainwater outflows so the water is flushed through regularly. Grow both from seed or stems rooted in water.

Harvest the young shoots of cattails (*Typha latifolia*) and eat like asparagus or pick the young leaves and stems from pickerel weed (*Pontederia cordata*) to eat raw or lightly steamed.

AQUATIC HERB GARDENS

Vietnamese coriander (*Persicaria odorata*) loves the shallows and has spicy young leaves for flavouring soups and spring rolls.

Water mint (*Mentha aquatica*) has a much stronger flavour than regular mint and makes good tea.

Sweet flag (*Acorus calamus*) has lemony leaves and fragrant, gingery rhizomes.

In Asian cultures, growing food in water is second nature (think rice paddies). So it's odd that edible aquatics are so overlooked in Western diets. There's a range of interesting nutritious greens and tubers you can grow in garden ponds – and you never have to remember to do the watering.

Q Are Brussels sprouts too big to grow in pots?

YOU CAN PICK A SMORGASBORD of fresh food from potted veg patches, from salads and leafy greens to chillies, tomatoes or French beans. But are there some vegetables you can't grow in pots? Are Brussels sprouts, for example, too big?

There are some veg you'll struggle to grow successfully in containers, but it's a small range: asparagus, sweetcorn, melons and rhubarb, mainly. Deep-rooted long carrots and parsnips grow stunted in containers, but you can get around that by growing parsnips in drainpipes (see page 189) or choosing stump-rooted carrots instead.

Some giants just grow a little less enormous in pots: purple sprouting broccoli and kale give you a decent harvest from large (60cm/2ft

MORE BIG VEG FOR SMALL SPACES

Courgette 'Patio Star'

Pea 'Tom Thumb'

Cauliflower 'Igloo'

Aubergine 'Ophelia' (pictured)

Cucumber 'Bush Champion'

A Modern breeding has powered a revolution in the way we grow veg. There are now pint-sized versions of nearly all the kitchen garden giants, from runner beans to raspberries, bringing even large plants like Brussels sprouts within range for veg gardeners confined to growing in containers.

WHAT ARE DWARF VEGETABLE VARIETIES?

Most vegetables grow naturally smaller if you plant them closer together: beetroots, cauliflowers and kale, for example (see page 118). Growing any naturally large plant in a pot stunts growth with a 'bonsai' effect. But the harvest usually suffers as a result: you'll either pick less or what you do pick will be smaller.

Truly dwarf vegetable varieties have been carefully bred to have smaller root systems that can handle the restricted environment of a container. Smaller roots mean less top growth, leaving more energy for flowers and fruit (or sprouts). So you pick surprisingly generous, normal-sized crops from a plant that's only knee high.

diameter) containers. Or just sow kale thickly across the container's surface and harvest as baby leaves.

Research varieties

Pay attention to the variety you choose and you really start expanding your container veg garden. While regular pumpkins quickly outgrow the limited resources in a pot, compact 'Baby Bear' reaches just 1.8m (6ft) across, producing lots of practically sized one-kilo (2lb) fruits. Dwarf runner bean 'Hestia' grows just 45cm (1½ft) tall before branching naturally and

erupting into flowers and bean pods. Calabrese 'Kabuki' grows half as high as other varieties and crops early – sow successively once a month through summer for a steady supply.

And there is a variety of Brussels sprout, 'Early Half Tall', about half the size of other sprouts at about 75cm (2½ft) tall. It produces its heavy crop sooner, so you can enjoy home-grown sprouts picked from your patio from mid-autumn onwards.

▶ Containers have a bonsai effect on kale and purple sprouting broccoli, so they grow naturally smaller but still give you a good harvest.

How can I get my hands on more growing space?

GARDENS ARE GETTING SMALLER and smaller these days, leaving little space for growing your own food. Many of us – about one in eight – don't have a garden at all. So what can you do about finding more land where you can expand your veg growing ambitions?

Allotments have always been a traditional refuge for frustrated vegetable growers. But these days they're so popular that waiting lists can run into decades. While you're waiting for the keys to a plot, get involved in community gardening in your area, or join a garden share scheme: as well as getting your hands into the soil at last, it's a great way to make new friends.

In the UK, councils are obliged by law to provide land to would-be gardeners in the form of allotments. Some sites are also owned privately by landlords, including the National Trust and the Church of England. So look up your local sites and visit to see which you like best, put your name down for a plot...and prepare for a long wait. It is still worth signing up: waiting lists are often shorter than expected as people lose interest or move away before they reach the top.

GARDEN SHARING

Before you start a garden share, agree on the rules, then get stuck in – it could be the start of a lifelong friendship. Factors to consider include:

• When is it convenient for you to spend time at the garden?

• Can you plant fruit trees or put up a greenhouse?

• How will you divide up the harvest?

• Who pays the bills for water or electricity?

• How will you communicate to iron out any problems?

Community gardening

Larger companies sometimes have workplace allotments for a spot of lunch-break gardening or you could even set up a site yourself if you know of a disused or neglected piece of land. Find the landowner and ask permission; you may find they're delighted to have it put to good use.

Volunteering at community gardens means you get to garden alongside other growers, so it's a good way to learn the ropes. You don't have as much say in what's grown, but you do take home a share of the produce. Community Supported Agriculture schemes are similar, but based on farms, so you get to look after animals, too.

Find your nearest community garden via the Federation of City Farms and Community Gardens (farmgarden.org.uk) or in the US, the American Community Gardening Association (communitygarden.org).

Garden sharing

Or you could stay closer to home and simply share someone else's garden. Ask around – you may find your neighbour is struggling and would appreciate the help. Or join a garden share scheme, matching wannabe gardeners with people with land to spare via apps and websites like allotme.co.uk and sharedearth.com.

◄ Allotments have a tradition of upcycling, recycling and making do, with plot holders often sharing seeds, plants and advice.

Do I have to grow my veg in rows?

THINK OF A TRADITIONAL VEG GARDEN and you're probably imagining serried ranks of well-behaved vegetables drawn up in arrow-straight lines, not a leaf out of place. But is that your only option? Do you have to grow veg in rows?

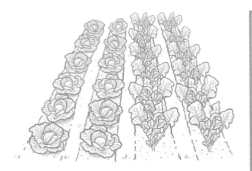

🔺 Monoculture growing is like hanging a big neon light over your crops for pests saying 'come and get me'!

Growing in rows is very practical, from a gardener's point of view: drawing long, straight drills is quick and efficient and you can get a hoe down the middle for weeding. Rows also keep each type of vegetable in one place, so they're more convenient to look after and easier to harvest.

But there are downsides. A whole row of vegetables is a lot of food when it's ready all at once. Also, the bare soil in between means a lot of wasted growing space. It's also easier for pests to find your veg when the crops are handily grouped together.

POLYCULTURE GROWING

Plants don't grow naturally in monocultures: in the wild they're all jumbled up in a joyous mix. Mimic natural polycultures by planting small patches of flowers, herbs, fruits and leaves, with larger plants like kale dotted singly here and there. Let salads, leaf beets, flowers and annual herbs self-seed, then replant any bare patches. You may have to cover brassicas with insect-proof mesh to fend off cabbage white caterpillars. Harvesting is more like foraging, but it's easy-going and completely in harmony with the environment.

Get creative!

So break free of the tyranny of straight rows and plant in triangles or zigzags – just for fun. Geometric, potager-style patterns can look as good as an ornamental garden, especially when you pair vegetables with different coloured leaves (red and green lettuces, say) or contrasting textures (smooth, slate-blue 'Bleu de Solaise' leeks look gorgeous grown among frothy 'Moss Curled' parsley).

Plant an edible carpet of low-growing salads and baby-leaf spinach under – or between – taller neighbours such as kale or broccoli to keep out weeds and lock moisture into the soil. Or just divide veg beds up into blocks and plant a different crop in each for small, manageable quantities of a wide variety of vegetables (see *What's Square Foot Gardening?*, page 216).

A We've been growing crops in rows for millennia. But the Victorians took the technique to heart, at a time when space was plentiful and time was cheap. Nowadays our veg plots must work harder, so grow in half-rows, blocks, patterns and groups to cover every inch of your soil with crops and to produce a more varied harvest.

You can also simply forget about geometry and plant wherever you can find a space. Cottage gardens are riots of veg, fruits, herbs and flowers, with few weeds; they need less watering, too.

Underplant brassicas with nasturtiums and dot other crops like chard into gaps to make sure every inch of your space is working hard.

Chapter 3

Incredible Edibles

Q How should I get my veg beds ready to plant?

GOOD SOIL IS THE FOUNDATION of every successful kitchen garden. So how do you make yours the best it can be ready for you to start the season?

WHAT DOES GOOD SOIL LOOK LIKE?

Good soil is deep and rich, with a dark brown colour, and extends 30–45cm (12–18in) below the surface. It's full of humus – the spongey remains of decayed vegetation – so it's very nutritious. It's also quite open-textured, so water drains through easily, but it still feels damp as humus holds moisture. Good soil crumbles when you break it up, and it's wriggling with life: you should bring up a few earthworms with every forkful.

A sk any question about soil and the answer is likely to involve organic matter. Adding this helps build a deep, rich topsoil as it works deep into the soil's structure, aerating sticky clay soils, so they don't get as waterlogged, and holding moisture and nutrients in light, free-draining sandy or chalky gardens.

Home-made garden compost from compost bins, wormeries and bokashi bins (see page 130) is best as it's free, makes good use of green waste and requires no transport. But it's hard to produce enough for larger veg gardens, so make up the shortfall with well-rotted farmyard manure, municipal green waste (from your local council) or biodigestate – leftover organic matter from biofuel plants. Source locally to cut transport miles and buy in loose loads when possible.

◀ Allow about half to one barrowload of mulch per square metre (3sq ft) of veg bed, and top it up every year.

KEEPING VEG BEDS SAFE IN WINTER

Protecting soil in winter is particularly important as relentless cold and heavy rain batter veg beds into hard pans, which are difficult to plant in spring and have all the nutrients sluiced out. Mulch thickly in autumn after clearing crops, to tuck your soil up under a protective blanket of organic matter. A cover of cardboard weighed down with bricks suppresses weeds, too.

Tree bark and wood chip mulch

Best preparation method

Hoe off winter weeds first; if you have problems with perennial weeds, covering the bed with some thick cardboard suppresses new growth through the season (see page 177). Then in spring, just before planting starts, spread organic matter over the top, 5–10cm (2–4in) deep.

Preparing veg beds for planting is the most important time you'll spend in the garden all year. Knock back weeds, so they don't outcompete vulnerable seedlings. Add long-lasting nutrients to boost your soil's subterranean ecosystem through mulching, to create perfect growing conditions.

There's no need to dig the organic matter in, as the worms do that for you. You can sow directly into mulches as long as they're very well-rotted (they should be fine, crumbly and shouldn't smell). If in doubt, raise veg separately under cover and grow as young plants. Repeat annually and the mulch will slowly blend deeper into the soil beneath, building a rich, thriving topsoil to fuel superbly healthy plants.

◤ Young plants get off to the best possible start when planted in rich soil that's well fed with annual mulches.

If I add sugar to the soil, will it make my tomatoes sweeter?

You'll hear lots of gardeners' tricks for making veg grow better. Some swear by burying banana skins or watering with cider vinegar. Others are adamant adding sugar to soil makes tomatoes grow sweeter. Is any of this true?

Plants are capable of producing sugar via photosynthesis, so adding it to soil makes no difference. Choose a sweeter tomato variety instead. It's true that sugar 'feeds' soil bacteria temporarily, but they die out after the initial sugar high. Organic mulches are more effective.

There's no scientific evidence that adding banana skins boosts flowers or fruit, and although vinegar is touted as a fertilizer and fungicide, it's also a key ingredient in organic weedkillers, which tells you all you need to know about how good it is for plants.

There's much tried-and-tested advice passed between gardeners. And there are a lot of myths that aren't backed up by science – like adding sugar to soil. So question everything, use common sense and experiment for yourself, only spending time and money on remedies you're sure work.

GARDEN HACKS

Bran against slugs
Unlike grit, eggshells and coffee grounds, bran isn't washed away into the soil when it rains: it swells instead, making barriers more effective.

Weeing on your garden
Well, perhaps not directly: dilute it 1:50 with water. Human urine is an extremely nitrogen-rich fertilizer – and you never run out.

Milk as a fungicide
Mix 50:50 of milk with water and spray on courgette leaves. In experiments milk was at least as effective as fungicidal sprays in preventing (not curing) mildew.

Is it worth thinning vegetable seedlings?

HOWEVER SPARINGLY YOU TRY TO SOW SEEDS, **a few come up in clumps. The traditional solution is thinning – removing unwanted seedlings. It seems a bit of a waste. Is there another approach?**

Station sowing cuts down on thinning by sowing seed at their final growing distance from the start. Instead of sprinkling seed along drills, make indents at the spacings you want and sow a few seeds into each, only thinning out to leave the strongest.

But for some veg, like beetroot, leeks, turnips and radish, you can skip thinning altogether and multi-sow instead. Multi-sowing deliberately grows vegetables in clumps instead of singly, so you harvest lots of baby veg over a longer time and from a smaller space – and you don't waste a single seed.

Beetroot,
Beta vulgaris

How to multi-sow

Sow three or four seeds to a module (newspaper pots work well – see page 74). Plant each cluster of seedlings outside in the garden just as they are, at normal final spacings. The seedlings push each other apart as they grow: once the largest reach harvestable size, carefully pull them out and leave the rest to grow on until you have harvested the whole clump.

Plants need space to grow, otherwise they compete with each other for nutrients and water and end up small, overcrowded and prone to fungal diseases. You can avoid thinning by station sowing, but you can also grow some veg in clumps for more plentiful crops from the same space.

How do I make my vegetables more nutritious?

GROWING YOUR OWN IS GOOD FOR YOU. It gets you out in the garden exercising – but most importantly you're growing fresh fruit and veg, packed with vitamins and minerals. But can you boost the health-giving properties of the food you grow?

There's huge variation in nutrient content between different types of the same vegetable. Sometimes specific varieties are better for you: one study found little-grown 'Jonathan' and 'Ontario' apples outscored 'Golden Delicious' and 'Braeburn' on disease-preventing antioxidants. Loose-leaf lettuce has higher calcium levels than romaine and baby plum tomatoes are highest in lycopene, which is linked to improved heart health.

Purple- or dark-skinned fruit and veg contain more anthocyanins, which help fend off cancer: so blueberries, blackcurrants, 'black' tomatoes like

'Indigo Rose' and purple varieties of carrot are particularly good for you. All are expensive or hard to find in the shops, but easy to grow at home.

Vegetables draw their mineral and vitamin content from the soil, so the richer your soil, the more nutritious the food that grows in it. Nitrogen is particularly good at boosting vitamin levels, so underplant crops with legumes like clover to fix nitrogen from the air into your soil.

How to boost nutrients

Cutting back on watering, so each plant gets just what it needs, increases levels of calcium, iron and potassium in fruits. It's important to harvest veg at the point of ripeness, when nutrient levels are at their peak. Nutrients – especially vitamins – start deteriorating the moment the plant is harvested, so only pick what you can eat straightaway. And cook carefully: vitamin C content stays intact in raw or steamed food, but you'll lose up to a third if you boil or microwave your veg instead.

The more fresh fruit and veg you eat, the healthier you'll be. But when it's grown at home, you can take the health-giving properties of your food to the max. What you grow, how you grow, and when (and how) you eat can all affect the nutritional value of your harvest.

HOME-GROWN SUPERFOODS

Blueberries One of the richest sources of anthocyanins and full of fibre.

Spinach Excellent source of iron, plus antioxidants like lutein for healthy eyes.

Beans Packed with protein and complex carbohydrates to keep you fuller for longer.

Kale Another good source of antioxidants and great for brain function.

Red peppers One red pepper has twice as much vitamin C as an orange.

Carrots Great source of beta-carotene, fibre, vitamin K, potassium...the list goes on.

Garlic Originally grown for medicine, garlic is a natural antibiotic and lowers blood pressure too.

Broccoli Naturally anti-inflammatory, helping lower the risk of stroke and heart disease.

Q What is leafmould?

IF YOU KICK THROUGH PILES OF AUTUMN LEAVES in your local woodland, you'll often find there's a deep, soft layer of dark, crumbly compost beneath. This is gardener's gold – also known as leafmould. What's so special about it?

Autumn leaves break down quite differently from other organic matter. In a compost bin, fast-acting bacteria do all the work, but leaves need fungi to rot, and it's a much slower process. That's why they're usually heaped up separately.

Leafmould is quite different from garden compost as it's very low in nutrients, fibrous and stable. It does the same job as peat in potting mixes, holding on to moisture while making the mix light and crumbly. It's perfect for sowing seeds, which need fewer nutrients while germinating. And if you have enough left over after making all that potting compost, it also makes an excellent mulch.

Leafmould is quite simply one of the most useful soil improvers there is. It's moisture-retentive, yet low in nutrients – invaluable for making potting mixes, especially for seed sowing. Yet you can't buy leafmould in the garden centre: the only way to get your hands on some is to make it yourself.

Which leaves?

You can make leafmould from any autumn leaves, but oak, beech and hornbeam break down the quickest. Sycamore and horse chestnut leaves have higher levels of lignin and decay more slowly: speed the process up by running the lawnmower over them to shred them.

Evergreen leaves are even slower: shred them and add to the compost heap, or compost separately (composted pine needles make a good acidic mulch for raspberries and blueberries).

Oak

Hornbeam

Beech

Leaves such as oak, beech and hornbeam are the best to use for leafmould as they break down quickly.

BUILD A LEAFMOULD BIN

- Find a sheltered, shady spot in the garden, ideally on grass or bare earth.

- Drive four 1.5m (5ft)-high fence posts into the ground, one in each corner of a 1m (3ft) square.

- Cut a length of 25mm (1in)-gauge chicken wire long enough to wrap round all four posts.

- Staple a batten to one end of the chicken wire, then, starting with the other end, attach it to all four posts. You are aiming to create a square bin with a 'door'.

- Wire the other end with the batten to the fourth post, so you can open it again to empty out the finished leafmould. Your bin is now ready to fill!

How to make leafmould

Pack your leaves into bin liners, or reusable builder's ('dumpy') bags, pierced with holes for drainage and dampen them if they're dry. If you have room, a bespoke leafmould bin (see above) allows you to make larger quantities. Within a year, you'll have a useful rough mulch for the garden; it's better to wait two years for the best-quality leafmould, fine enough for seed compost if sieved first.

Tread leaves down as you fill the bag to fit in as many as possible; you'll find the level drops as the leaves break down.

Does pinching out tomatoes really help?

PINCHING OUT IS A WEEKLY CHORE when you're growing tomatoes: you work your way up each stem in turn, nipping out sideshoots between finger and thumb. But does it really help your tomatoes – or can you get away without doing it?

Tomatoes left to their own devices grow into a jungly mass of lush green growth, romping around in a riot of unmanageable foliage – and relatively few, quite small fruits.

Pinching out the sideshoots so they can't develop reduces tomato plants to a single stem. This makes them easier to support and you're able to get into your greenhouse (always a plus). It also concentrates the plant's energies into producing fruit rather than foliage. The result is a neater tomato plant and fewer but much larger fruits.

HOW TO TRAIN A DOUBLE CORDON

- Plant your tomato between two sturdy supports, one on each side.

- Let the tomato grow until it has produced one good, strong sideshoot.

- Tie the leading shoot to one support and the sideshoot to the other.

- Pinch out further sideshoots from both stems as they appear, tying them to their supports as they grow.

CAN I GROW TOMATOES WITHOUT A GREENHOUSE?

Tomatoes are the most widely grown greenhouse crop, with good reason. Greenhouses provide extra warmth for ripening fruit and shelter leaves from rain – so they're safe from the devastating fungal disease late blight, which is carried in raindrops.

However, even if you don't have a greenhouse, you can still grow tomatoes – just choose the right varieties. You want toms that are early to ripen and naturally blight-resistant: 'Latah', 'Mountain Magic' and container tom 'Losetto' are all equally good grown outside as under glass.

The only way to avoid pinching out tomatoes is to grow bush varieties. But they almost all produce cherry-sized fruits, so to enjoy the full range of varieties, it's worth going to the effort of growing cordon types, which must be trained and pinched out to fruit well.

As well as pinching out sideshoots, it's also wise to pinch out the topmost growing tip once the plant reaches the roof of the greenhouse or (outside) the top of its supports: this is practical, as it stops the plant continuing to grow upwards, but also helps direct the plant's resources into ripening fruit at the end of the season.

Double-stemmed cordons

There is a compromise, though. While you'll get the largest fruits from single cordons, double-stemmed cordons give you many more tomatoes from the same plant. They will be slightly smaller but the difference is hardly noticeable – so you'll almost double your harvest.

Bush variety   Cordon variety

How do I know my seeds are still alive?

SEEDS ARE SLEEPING BEAUTIES: baby plants in suspended animation waiting for that ideal moment when soil temperature and moisture are just right to bring them back to life. But is that guaranteed? How do you know your seeds are still alive?

As a general rule, most seeds begin to lose viability and the germination rate starts to fall after about two years in storage. So where you might have had 90 percent germinate when you first collected or bought the seed, after three years just 70–80 percent will come up, declining year on year as the seed gets older.

This varies from seed to seed. Longer-lived seeds include beans, tomatoes, brassicas, cucumbers and

TESTING SEED VIABILITY

Test the viability of older seed with a simple pre-germination test:

- Lay kitchen roll in a tray and dampen with water.

- Sprinkle a few seeds on top, then wrap loosely in a plastic bag.

- Place somewhere warm – an airing cupboard is ideal – and check daily.

- Keep damp.

- If the seeds germinate after three or four days, you're good to sow.

Cucumbers are among several types of seed that keep really well and germinate readily, even after several years in storage.

WHY HAVEN'T MY SEEDS GERMINATED?

Seed doesn't germinate if it's sown into soil that's too cold (below 10°C/50°F) or too hot (lettuce seed struggles above 21°C/70°F). Letting seeds dry out or waterlogging them is usually fatal too. Some just take their time: parsley and parsnips often take over a month to appear. You may find that even if they germinate, slugs and mice eat seedlings as they emerge, so you never get near them. Sow under cover, then transplant outside as young plants instead.

Parsley (*Petroselinum crispum*) seedlings

melons, which often germinate well at up to eight years old. Carrots, parsnips, onions, leeks, parsley and parsnips have a much shorter lifespan – no more than two or three years.

Seed storage

Seeds also live longer if you store them well. Seeds keep longest somewhere cool (about 5°C/40°F), dry and dark. If you collect your own seed into paper envelopes, place them in an airtight container, ideally with a desiccant sachet – often found in packaging for clothing – and keep them in the fridge (though a cool spare room will do). If you buy your seed, you can just leave it in the sealed packet as long as it's kept somewhere cool and dry. Remember to

sort through your packeted seed every couple of years and throw out any that are too old, so you keep germination rates as high as possible.

Seeds quickly lose viability (the ability to germinate) if they get too old or are stored badly. Some are more sensitive than others: carrot and parsnip seeds, for example, start dying after just a year, while five-year-old tomato seeds often germinate happily. A simple test can tell you if seeds are still viable (see opposite).

Should I grow maincrop or baby veg?

Baby cos lettuce, *Lactuca sativa* 'Little Gem'

IT CAN FEEL LIKE AN AWFUL LONG WAIT until your full-sized, maincrop veg are ready. But you don't always have to wait: many crops are good harvested while still immature, to eat as baby veg. But which is best?

Baby veg are as nutritious as the full-sized versions, but very different in texture and flavour. Maincrop veg are richly flavoured and full of fibre; baby veg are tender and crisp, with a more delicate flavour.

Use baby veg for early (and late) sowings to extend your harvest. You can also snatch a harvest from the space between larger crops, like kale or sprouts, while they mature. You can even grow baby beetroot, round-rooted carrots and radishes on the windowsill.

Baby veg are fantastic in small spaces and containers as they grow quickly and take up little room. But maincrop veg give you a higher overall yield – so if you have the space, grow both. Maincrop veg provide the bulk, while baby veg deliver a steady stream of delicately flavoured treats.

BABY VEG FOUR WAYS

Harvest early
Pull beetroot and turnips at golf ball size and 'fingerling' carrots when shoulders are about 1cm (^{1}/2in) wide.

Choose dwarf varieties
Mini versions include 'Tom Thumb' lettuces, 'Paris Market' carrots and 'Tokyo Cross' turnips.

Sow close together
Plant summer cauliflowers and calabrese at half spacings, 15–20cm (6–8in) apart, for half-sized crops.

Leave plants in the ground
Broccoli and cabbage stumps resprout after harvesting the main head, producing sweet baby shoots.

Can I compost my weeds?

AFTER AN ENTHUSIASTIC BOUT OF WEEDING the garden looks great, but you have a heap of surplus greenery on your hands. Is it safe to put it all in the compost bin?

Not only is it safe to compost your weeds – you should. Every weed you remove is organic matter you're taking from the soil and composting is one way to put it back again. You can even compost perennial weed roots and seeds – after special treatment – so they don't come back to haunt you.

Annual weeds hoed off early, before they've set seed, and perennial weed top growth can go straight onto the compost heap just as they are. You can also shred woody weeds such as brambles before adding those, too.

A hot compost heap, cooking at 60°C or more (140°F), kills both weed seeds and roots. But most ordinary garden compost bins are cold. In this case, kill weed seeds and perennial roots before adding them (see right), or they may survive the composting process and resprout when you spread the compost as mulch.

COMPOSTING PERENNIAL WEED ROOTS AND SEEDS

Remove leafy growth and add straight to the compost bin.

Put roots and seeds into a dustbin, cover with water and leave for six weeks.

Decant the liquid off to use as feed (see page 124) and add the remains to your compost.

Alternatively, **spread roots out** in the sunshine – ideally on corrugated iron – and leave to bake for a week. Once they're brittle and snap easily, they are dead and you can safely compost them.

Q My container crops are looking sick – what can I do?

VEG IN POTS ARE MOSTLY TROUBLE-FREE and escape many of the problems that beset crops in the ground. But sometimes things do go wrong – so how do you know what's afflicting your container crops and what can you do about it?

In many ways, growing veg in containers helps protect them. There aren't any soil-borne diseases in fresh compost and pots are easy to move out of rain, avoiding blight, rust and peach leaf curl. But containers are artificial environments, where roots can't stretch out as they would in soil to explore for nutrients and water. So potted veg patches are dependent on you for their needs – and if you get it wrong, they quickly get sick.

Check for pests

Watch out for slugs, aphids and blackfly, which adore tender bean shoots. Notched leaves could mean

THREE-POINT HEALTH CHECK FOR CONTAINER VEG

1 Shoot tips should be perky: if they're puckered and distorted, suspect aphids and squish on sight.

2 Leaves should be green and clean: yellowing leaves may mean lack of feed, while holes could be slugs or vine weevils.

3 Stems should be upright: wilting can be a sign of drought or waterlogging. Strawberries also wilt when vine weevil grubs are at work on the roots.

▼ Group plants together in large containers if you can – the bigger your pots, the easier they are to keep watered and fed.

When watering containers, a good soak is better than a light sprinkle: water until the excess runs out of the bottom of the pot.

Slugs, aphids and rain-borne diseases – like late blight – affect plants in pots just as much as in the open garden. Vine weevil can be a real pain in pots, too. But often when container veg look sick it's down to stress, usually because they're not getting the essentials they need.

vine weevils are about: their C-shaped grubs can eat the roots right off strawberries (see page 163). Water on biological controls from midsummer, before they do serious harm. Fend off slugs and snails by raising pots on pot feet above saucers of water: slugs don't like to swim and usually opt for an easier meal instead.

Feed and water well

Normal multipurpose potting compost contains enough nutrients to last about six weeks. After that it's up to you to give crops a weekly liquid feed throughout the season. Erratic watering is also a major cause of yellowing leaves, wilting stems and poor growth. Stick your finger deep into the compost: if you can't feel damp, the pot needs more water.

Overwatering is just as dangerous: if the compost feels soggy rather than damp, stop watering and lift your pots up on pot feet or bring them under shelter to let them dry out.

On very hot days, move your pots temporarily into shade or cover them with a sheet to keep the sun off, so the compost doesn't dry out as quickly. Water on rainy days too; light rain often barely wets the compost's surface, so it's easy for pots to dry out without you noticing.

Plants in pots are easier to protect from diseases carried in rainwater, like late blight. Move pots under cover, so the foliage stays dry.

Do I need to pollinate my greenhouse crops?

BEES, HOVERFLIES AND OTHER POLLINATORS are your friends in the veg garden, essential for producing about a third of your crops. But how do they find their way inside a greenhouse? And if they can't, should you pollinate your greenhouse crops yourself?

Tomatoes, peppers and aubergines are self-fertile and can pollinate their own flowers. But pollen is released only when the flowers are vibrated, usually by the buzzing of a bumblebee. Gently tapping each flower in turn mimics this and helps fruit set, though encouraging bees into your greenhouse is less time-consuming.

A soft artist's paintbrush picks up pollen just as a bee would and transfers it onto another flower.

HOW TO HAND-POLLINATE

• Wait until you have several flowers that are fully open.

• Take a soft artist's paintbrush and dab it into the centre of a flower: this transfers a dusting of yellow pollen onto the brush.

• Dab the brush gently into another flower, repeating until you've pollinated all the flowers.

• Do this every couple of days until the petals fall off and you see the developing fruit behind.

Melons won't produce fruit at all if they aren't pollinated, so make sure insects can get into the greenhouse or hand-pollinate the flowers yourself. Spring-flowering greenhouse fruit like strawberries forced under cover for an early crop, or apricots and peaches in polytunnels, need hand-pollinating too, as there aren't many insects around at that time of year.

Natural pollinators

Encourage insects to come inside by opening the vents and doors wide on sunny days. Grow colourful, nectar-rich flowers such as marigolds and nasturtiums in pots outside the door (to attract insects towards the greenhouse) and among your crops (to lure them in).

But in truth, insects are getting harder to coax into a greenhouse these days simply because there are fewer of them: insect numbers are in long-term decline due to a combination of climate change, habitat loss and

GREENHOUSE CUCUMBERS

Greenhouse cucumbers don't need pollinating – they're better without. Allow greenhouse cucumbers to cross-pollinate and the fruits turn bitter, so pollination is to be discouraged: pick off male flowers (those with a straight stem behind, rather than a baby fruit) every few days before they can pollinate the females. Or just save yourself the bother and buy an all-female variety that doesn't produce male flowers.

pesticide use. So a dual approach is best: provide plenty of nectar to lure in bees, but pollinate your crops yourself as well, just in case.

Most greenhouse crops can pollinate their own flowers or produce fruit without. But some crops must be pollinated and others fruit better if they are. So encouraging pollinators into the greenhouse, or doing it yourself, usually boosts your harvest.

Golden marigold,
Calendula officinalis

How can I make my own fertilizers?

SYNTHETIC FERTILIZERS have a sky-high carbon footprint and even organic fertilizers usually come packaged in hard-to-recycle plastic bottles. So it's much better for the environment if you can make your own. But how?

If you're looking after the soil well, using generous mulches, plants in the ground should have all the nutrients they need. Container veg and greenhouse crops do need extra feeding, but you needn't buy fertilizers: make all you need from materials already growing in your garden.

Liquid feeds give an instant pick-me-up to all plants, added to the watering can once a week in summer. Any plant material makes good liquid feed, but two are particularly useful: nettles – which are high in nitrogen – and potassium-packed comfrey.

MORE HOME-MADE FERTILIZERS

Wood ash Alkaline, so use with care, but high in potassium.

Seaweed Ask permission before collecting and rinse in fresh water before using.

Coffee grounds Acidic, but full of nutrients – use sparingly as too much inhibits growth.

Eggshells Grind or crush finely, then add to soil for calcium.

Borage Good, all-round, nitrogen-rich fertilizer, similar to comfrey.

Comfrey leaves are high in potassium, which encourages plenty of fruit, so comfrey tea makes a good natural substitute for tomato food.

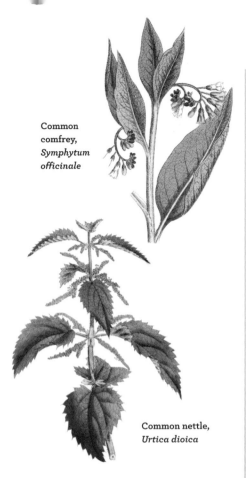

Common
comfrey,
*Symphytum
officinale*

Common nettle,
Urtica dioica

Making your fertilizer

Pick nettles while young to catch
them at peak nitrogen content and
grow a special comfrey patch to
harvest by cutting leaves to just above
ground level two or three times a year.
Ordinary comfrey can be invasive, so
plant the variety 'Bocking 14' as this
is better behaved and doesn't
self-seed around your garden.

The method is the same for both.
Pack leaves into a bucket (the more
you cram in, the richer the fertilizer),
weigh down with a brick and cover
with water. Leave to steep for a

month – a lid is useful, since it can
get quite smelly.

Decant the resulting brown liquid
into bottles. Dilute the feed before
using: it isn't an exact science, as the
strength of home-made liquid feeds
can be very variable, but as a rule of
thumb the diluted feed should be
the colour of weak tea.

BREW COMPOST TEA

Extract the nutrients from
compost, then turbo-charge
them in aerated water to
make compost tea.

• Tip a spadeful of compost
  into a hessian bag and tie
  the top.

• Fill a bucket with rainwater
  and add five tablespoons
  of sugar or molasses.

• Lower an aquarium air pump
  (ideally solar-powered) into
  the water and switch it on.

• Hang the hessian bag from a
  cane balanced over the top of
  the bucket, so it's submerged.

• Leave the tea to brew for two
  days (it will bubble and froth
  enthusiastically) – use fresh
  and undiluted.

How much should I be feeding my veg plants?

VEGETABLES NEED JUST THE RIGHT COMBINATION of minerals and trace elements to give their best. It's up to you as the gardener to make sure they get them. But how do you know what and how much to feed your plants?

Adding lots of compost to your soil doesn't feed it directly, as organic matter is relatively low in nutrients. But it does massively improve the soil's structure, and that in turn builds a vibrant subterranean ecosystem – which then feeds your plants.

It takes up to five years to build up your soil, though. So for the first year or two on a new veg plot, help things along by scattering organic slow-release fertilizer like seaweed meal before mulching in spring. No extra feed should be needed: in fact,

Leafy veg like lettuces in containers or the winter greenhouse love a dose of nitrogen-rich nettle tea once a week.

overfeeding makes crops susceptible to diseases like rust and blossom end rot in tomatoes.

In containers, it's a different story. Ordinary multipurpose potting compost contains enough nutrients to keep plants going for about six weeks, but after that start adding liquid feeds (see page 124) to the watering can once a week. You can also add well-rotted manure to the lower half of pots before topping with multipurpose compost for a long-lasting nutrient boost for your container veg.

Most healthy soil contains enough nutrients for normal growth, so if you're looking after your soil well, adding extra fertilizer is generally unnecessary. Concentrate your efforts on crops in greenhouses or containers, which depend solely on you for their nutrient needs.

YEAR-ROUND FEEDING SCHEDULE

Spring

- Mulch beds generously, adding seaweed meal to new beds.

- Harvest comfrey and nettles and set aside to steep in water.

- Put compost tea on to brew.

- Feed growing seedlings with half-strength liquid seaweed or compost tea.

Summer

- Start weekly liquid feeds six weeks after planting veg in containers.

- Feed greenhouse crops weekly as soon as they're planted out.

- Switch to targeted feeds halfway through the season as crops mature.

Autumn

- Stop feeding as crops start winding down.

- Add wood ash to beds where you'll grow brassicas next year.

- Mulch (without extra feed) ready for winter.

Choose the right feed

Choose the right feed for the job: all-rounder feeds like liquid seaweed or compost tea are ideal at the start of the season, but as crops mature switch to something more targeted. Nitrogen-rich nettle tea encourages leafy lettuces, spinach and kale, while potassium-rich comfrey feed boosts fruits in tomatoes, aubergines and cucumbers. Always feed onto damp compost: plants can't take up feeds properly from dry soil and it may cause nutrient deficiencies. Stop feeding at the end of summer, as your crops are winding down by then and don't need it.

Keep greenhouse cucumbers healthy with weekly feeds of seaweed, followed by comfrey tea once the flowers open.

Do I have to do lots of digging?

YOU'LL STILL FIND VEGETABLE GROWERS who swear by the traditional practice of double digging the plot from one end to the other every autumn, working manure deep into the ground. It sounds like an awful lot of hard work – is it really necessary?

Putting away the spade and relying on mulches instead is a lot less work – and it turns your veg patch into a mini carbon sink as you feed carbon-rich organic matter continuously into the soil. That then turbo-charges the billions of organisms that live unseen beneath

your feet; left undisturbed they form myriad relationships between each other and your plants, helping roots plug into soil nutrients and moisture more easily.

Start your no-dig garden by scalping the area, mowing off grass or weeds (no need to dig them up, though do cut out the crowns of woody brambles). Then cover with a layer of cardboard, topped with a really thick mulch – about 10–15cm (4–6in) deep.

A no-dig system is particularly useful for heavy clay as you leave the underlying soil undisturbed and plant into the mulches on top – so root veg find it much easier to grow.

Experiments comparing dug and undug plots have now shown that vegetables grow at least as well without digging – and sometimes better. So all that back-breaking work doesn't achieve much: in fact, it can do more harm than good as digging demolishes the soil's fragile ecosystem, as well as contributing to climate change.

WHERE TO GET YOUR MULCH

The most challenging part of no-dig gardening is getting your hands on enough organic matter. Make as much as you can yourself, then source the rest as locally as possible.

Garden compost
Free and the greenest option, but it's almost impossible to make enough.

Municipal green waste
Recycled garden waste from your local council, thoroughly treated to kill off any weed seeds or disease.

Farmyard manure
Plunder muck heaps at local farms and riding stables, but check first that pasture hasn't been treated with herbicides as these can contaminate compost.

 Manure should be rotted down for a year before you use it on the garden – if in doubt, add it to the compost heap instead.

Biodigestate
Some farms run biofuel energy plants and the residue makes a highly nutritious, fine-textured mulch.

Maintaining your mulch

You can plant and sow straight into mulch as long as it's really well-rotted, with a fine texture like breadcrumbs. Sieve rougher mulches or just compost them for a little longer until they've broken down properly. This first, deep mulch will get you started, then after that you just need to top up with a further layer, 5–8cm (2–3in) thick, every year in either autumn or spring.

You get fewer weeds when you stop digging, and you don't need to water as much, as mulches lock in moisture, too. Even clearing spent crops is easier as you just cut them away at ground level, leaving roots to rot naturally and add even more organic matter to the soil. It's veg growing, but without the hard graft – leaving you free to get on with the fun stuff like sowing and planting.

How do I make compost without a compost bin?

MAKING COMPOST IS FREE. It helps your plants grow better and it's upcycling waste – which is great for the environment, too. But what if your garden is too small for a compost bin – or you have no garden at all? Can you still make compost?

The minimum size for a conventional compost heap is 90cm (35in) square – and if your garden is small, that's a big sacrifice. But there are other ways to turn kitchen scraps into feed for your plants.

Wormeries

These harness red brandling worms to turn kitchen scraps (including cooked food, though not meat or dairy) into worm wee, an excellent liquid fertilizer. You can buy wormeries from specialist stockists or make one yourself. Keep wormeries indoors or in a sheltered spot outside. Once your worms have settled in, add 5–10cm (2–4in) of scraps at a time. Drain off the liquid for feeding your plants and remove compost to use in the garden or as a mulch for containers.

Bokashi bins

A Japanese innovation, these use fermentation to turn all kitchen food waste – apart from bones – into "pre-compost". You then add this to wormeries or compost bins, or simply mix into garden soil where it will break down further.

🔻 It's important not to add too much kitchen waste at once to your wormery – just add a layer at a time, so the worms can keep up.

Traditional slatted compost bins are fine if you have room – but there are lots of other options that take up less space, or even none at all. Recycle your kitchen and garden waste in wormeries, bokashi bins or even straight into the ground and you can make compost wherever you live.

Bokashi bins are lidded buckets, small enough to fit neatly onto the kitchen counter.

Add waste in layers, compress to exclude air, then scatter with a handful of inoculated bokashi bran (available from specialist suppliers). Once the bin is full, seal and leave for two weeks, draining off surplus liquid occasionally (if you have two bins on the go, you can be filling one while the other is fermenting). The resulting pickled waste is packed with beneficial micro-organisms to boost plant growth.

In-garden composting

Forget compost bins and just compost straight into the ground. Dig trenches about 30cm (12in) deep for climbing beans, or pits 60–90cm (20–35in) deep and wide for pumpkins, courgettes and tomatoes. Line with newspaper, then build up layers of kitchen scraps and green waste, covering each layer with soil so the scraps don't attract vermin. Once you reach the top, leave to rot down over winter, then top up with soil ready to plant next spring.

LASAGNE GARDENS

Create a lasagne garden and you can compost straight onto the ground. Lay newspaper or cardboard down first, then build layers of green waste followed by compost or soil until you have a raised bed 25–30cm (10–12in) high, ending with a compost or soil layer. Leave it to rot over winter and the bed will be ready to plant in spring. Below are some ideas for the green waste layers in your lasagne garden, each separated by a layer of compost or soil.

Add a layer of compost or soil between each main layer

Planting layer (topsoil)

Manure

Food waste

Straw

Manure

Grass clippings

Cardboard or newspaper

Underlying soil

Help! My compost has turned gloopy!

YOU'VE FILLED YOUR COMPOST BIN with grass clippings and vegetable peelings, left it a month or two – and now it's turned to revolting, smelly slime. It's no good for putting on the vegetable garden, so what's gone wrong?

Compost turns anaerobic when it gets too wet and liquid fills all the air pockets, driving out oxygen. Sometimes that's because you've added too much lush green material, but it also happens if it's sodden with rain or you've forgotten to turn your heap. You'll have the opposite problem if you add too much fibrous material without any greenery: with more air than organic matter bacteria can't work effectively and the bin contents just sit there without rotting.

The bacteria responsible for good garden compost thrive in the presence of air. Lush greenery collapses as it breaks down, becoming compacted and airless. Add too much at once, without any fibre to hold it open, and anaerobic bacteria take over instead – and they work differently, turning everything into a wet, stagnant mess with a nasty smell.

Getting a balance

The sweet spot is a 50:50 balance of fast-rotting 'greens' (including farmyard manure and kitchen scraps as well as grass clippings and weeds) and slow-rotting 'browns' (fibrous

If you have lots of greenery to add to your compost bin, mix in drier materials such as straw, shredded newspaper or wood shavings to keep it well aerated.

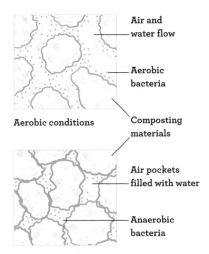

Aerobic conditions

Air and water flow

Aerobic bacteria

Composting materials

Air pockets filled with water

Anaerobic bacteria

Anaerobic conditions

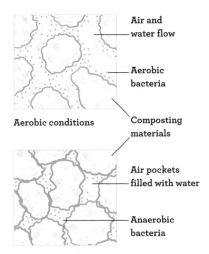 Aerobic bacteria can't survive without air, so in airless heaps anaerobic bacteria take over, releasing methane and hydrogen sulphide.

stems, torn-up newspaper, straw or shredded prunings).

Avoid adding too much of any one ingredient all at once: if you have large quantities of grass clippings, mix in some browns as you're adding them to your heap. Stir things up further by turning your compost at least once, and ideally two or three times during the year, forking everything out before forking it back in again.

Compost turned once or twice is finished within nine months to a year: sooner if you turn it more often. You'll know the compost is ready when it's dark brown and crumbly, without any individual ingredients visible: it's now ready to spread on your garden.

HOW TO RESCUE GLOOPY COMPOST

Even slimy, smelly compost can be revived with a little time and effort.

• Dig out your compost heap completely, removing all the gloopy material.

• Line the empty bin with a 5cm (2in) layer of fibrous material like straw.

• Add a 5cm (2in) layer of gloopy compost on top, and fork over lightly to mix it in.

• Add another layer of straw or shredded newspaper, followed by a layer of bad compost and repeat until it has all been returned to the compost bin.

• Leave the compost to rot, turning two or three times during the year. Once you've turned your compost bin, cover it with cardboard weighed down with bricks so it doesn't get waterlogged in winter – this will keep weed seeds out, too.

Do home-made pest remedies really work?

ONE OF THE BEST REASONS FOR GROWING YOUR OWN FOOD is knowing it's never been sprayed with pesticides. But how do you protect your crops without using pesticides? What about using home-made remedies – do they really work?

THREE REMEDIES TO TRY AT HOME...

Garlic spray Insect repellent – though mixed reports on effectiveness: experiment with higher concentrations if it doesn't work at first.

Garlic, *Allium sativum*

Chilli water Insect repellent that infuses plant leaves with capsaicin, making them unpalatable.

Tomato leaves Contain toxic compounds capable of repelling and sometimes killing sap-sucking insects.

Tomato leaves

...AND THREE TO AVOID

Eggshells Supposed to keep slugs off lettuces, but tests have shown they just slime right over them.

Rhubarb water Effective pesticide, but kills everything and contains oxalic acid – poisonous to adults.

Diatomaceous earth Soft, silica-rich sedimentary rock that dehydrates insects and slugs, but stops working when it gets wet.

Home-made pesticides are far kinder to the environment: being plant-derived, they don't leave harmful residues in soil and watercourses. They're low-carbon, milder (so often need frequent re-applying) and don't come packed in hard-to-recycle plastic.

However, many remedies are handed down from gardener to gardener, without ever having been put through rigorous scientific testing. So it's sometimes hard to tell which remedies genuinely protect your crops and which are just folklore.

Proven protection

A few have come out well in scientific studies: experiments have shown that milk, for example, prevents mildew in courgette leaves at least as well as synthetic fungicides. And many remedies are based on sound science: garlic contains sulphurous compounds unpalatable to insects, while capsaicin – the ingredient that makes chilli peppers hot – is a proven insect repellent.

It's worth bearing in mind, though, that home-made insecticides are indiscriminate and repel or kill ladybirds as well as aphids. So start by preventing pests damaging your crops in the first place (see *Chapter 4 What's Eating My Crops?* for suggestions) and reach for the spray bottle only in emergencies – when pests have breached your defences and are causing serious trouble.

Some plants come armed with natural defences against pests and diseases. Capture these to make home-made pesticides and they'll often work as well as any shop-bought spray. But claims about how well they work are rarely backed by scientific evidence, so do plenty of research and be prepared to experiment.

HOW TO MAKE HOME-MADE PESTICIDES

• Roughly chop a generous handful of fresh ingredients.

• Tip into a 1 litre (2 pint) jar and fill with water.

• Leave to steep overnight (tomato leaves and garlic) or up to a week (chillies).

• Strain through muslin into a clean bowl.

• Add a tablespoon of liquid Castile soap and decant into your spray bottle.

Chilli, *Capsicum frutescens*

Can other plants help my veg grow better?

PLANTS IN THE WILD RARELY GROW IN ISOLATION. They're part of a community, jostling for space with other plants alongside. But are they competing with or supporting one another? Could growing with other plants help my vegetables grow better?

BUILDING A GUILD

Guilds are made up of several different elements, all woven together:

Fertilizers Legumes (peas and beans, plus clover, lupins and sea buckthorn) can 'fix' nitrogen from the air into the soil via bacteria living on their roots – feeding plants growing nearby, too.

Common chicory, *Cichorium intybus*

Living mulches Large-leaved plants like squash shade the ground so it stays damp longer. They also stop weeds taking hold.

Mining plants Plants with long taproots draw up micronutrients from deep in the ground for other plants to use. Carrots, parsnips and fruit trees do this well, as do chicory, dandelion and sorrel.

Pollinator magnets Pollinating insects boost harvests and prey on pests. Sunflowers, marigolds, nasturtiums and flowering herbs bring your veg patch to life.

Winter squash, *Cucurbita maxima*

Evidence is now growing that plants form partnerships to benefit each other. You can mimic those beneficial effects in the garden by planting in 'guilds' – groups of plants that like similar conditions and grow happily together, helping each other out with everything from shade and fertilizer to pest control.

The concept of a 'guild' is borrowed from ecologists, who use it to describe plants that occupy similar environments, growing alongside each other and using more or less the same resources.

Vegetables grown in guilds mimic natural guilds by grouping plants together so that each plant brings something to the party. The result is a happy harmony in which each plant plays its part in repelling pests, making nutrients available to other plants, suppressing weeds and generally keeping the community strong and healthy just as nature intended, without you having to do a thing.

When you grow in guilds you plant up to a dozen different crops in each bed, each one carefully chosen to co-operate with rather than compete with the others. The result is a rounded, vibrant ecosystem that provides plenty of good food for you to eat.

EXAMPLE OF A GUILD

- **Apple tree** Feeds pollinators and brings up minerals.

- **Blackcurrant** Wind protection and attracts pollinators.

- **French beans** Nitrogen fixer, nectar-rich flowers.

- **Courgette** Living mulch, nectar-rich flowers.

- **Beetroot** Roots draw up nutrients; flowers attract pollinators.

- **Onion** Natural pest deterrent.

- **Carrots** Mine minerals; allow a few to flower for insects.

- **Oregano** Flowers are adored by pollinators.

- **Nasturtium** Salad ingredient and attracts pollinators, living mulch.

- **Dandelions** Mine minerals, feed pollinators, good to eat when blanched.

- **Pot marigolds** Attract insects, edible flowers.

- **Clover** Nitrogen fixer, living mulch.

White clover,
*Trifolium
repens*

How can marigolds help my tomatoes grow?

CARPETS OF MARIGOLDS BENEATH YOUR TOMATOES **add a splash of colour to the greenhouse – but are they more than just pretty flowers? Can marigolds help your tomatoes grow better?**

Companion planting – pairing plants to help one or both grow better – is an old gardening tradition that can help protect your plants from pests without having to resort to pesticides. But much of the evidence is anecdotal and hasn't been properly tested, so it's best to turn scepticism settings to high and be prepared to experiment.

The most valuable companion pairings are the few that have undergone scientific testing – like marigolds and tomatoes. The smell emitted by French marigolds is limonene, the same chemical found in citrus peel, and it's been shown to put off all sorts of insects (it's also used in mosquito repellents).

Sow *Tagetes* from seed in early spring, with a little extra heat from a propagator or warm windowsill.

If you've ever brushed against a French marigold (*Tagetes patula*) you'll know they have a strong, peculiar smell – bitter, pungent and grassy. This repels whitefly, keeping your tomatoes safe right through the season. Plant generously for maximum impact: they'll help keep weeds down, too.

Cabbages and clover

Another study showed pests, such as cabbage root fly and cabbage white butterflies, lay fewer eggs on cabbages underplanted with clover – though laying green card on the ground produced a similar effect, suggesting it's more about how insects find their target than about specific combinations.

There's less evidence that planting onions near carrots helps deter carrot fly (try growing them under insect-proof mesh instead), or that growing the thyme-like herb summer savory near broad beans repels blackfly (nipping the growing tips out in early summer does a better job).

Using 'decoy' plants as companions can be effective: nasturtiums lure blackfly away from broad beans, for example. But remember to uproot the nasturtiums, with their load of blackfly, before the insects have reduced them to rags, run out of food and returned to your beans in even greater numbers.

The common-sense approach

Just because tests haven't been carried out doesn't necessarily mean companion planting doesn't work. But rather than focusing too closely on specific plant pairings, a broader, more common-sense approach is likely to be more successful. Plant any kind of nectar-rich flowers among crops, for instance, to lure in natural predators and reduce your aphid population. They'll look lovely, too!

BAD COMPANIONS

Some plants are allelopaths – they emit chemicals from the roots that actively prevent other plants growing well nearby. Walnut trees are well-known allelopaths: fennel and garlic also inhibit the growth of neighbouring plants.

But even bad companions are sometimes helpful. Tall, leafy Mexican marigolds (*Tagetes minuta*) emit such strong chemicals from their roots they stop even perennial weeds growing: plant on land infested by bindweed, ground elder and couch grass as a natural weedkiller.

Fennel,
Foeniculum vulgare

Will my veg taste better if eaten the moment they are picked?

YOU'VE CAREFULLY TENDED YOUR PLANTS ALL SEASON from seed to mature plant – and now at last they're ready to pick. But how should you time it to max out on flavour? Is it true home-grown veg taste better if you eat them straightaway?

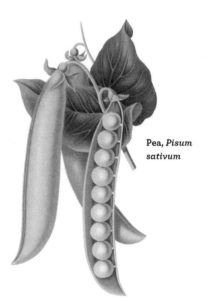

Pea, *Pisum sativum*

can, eat fresh veg right after picking. But while fresh is best, sometimes it's just not possible to pick and eat straightaway. And that's fine, too – your veg will still taste great as long as you pop it straight in the fridge and eat within a few days.

Good keepers

There are also exceptions. Tomatoes and strawberries carry on developing sugars after harvesting, so can taste even better if left at room temperature for a day or two after picking.

Picking fruit and pods at peak ripeness captures your harvest when levels of sugar and other flavour compounds are at their highest, so it tastes as good as it can. But the very act of picking triggers a chain reaction.

In some veg, sugars and other flavour compounds start breaking down straightaway; others switch to emergency mode and start converting sugars into longer-lasting but less pleasant-tasting starches. Neither reaction is good for flavour: so if you

The moment you pick fruit, pods and leaves you remove their source of energy and water. In most cases, that affects texture – as leaves lose moisture and wilt – and flavour. This continues even through refrigeration, so to enjoy your harvest at its best, get it onto your plate as soon as you can.

Which veg taste better if you grow them yourself?

FOR SOME VEG – onions, for example – there's not a lot of difference in flavour between home-grown and shop-bought. But for others, the flavour when you grow them yourself is in a different league. So which veg are best home-grown?

Those veg we eat while still young, or lush and leafy, have few defences and don't survive long when removed from the plant. Baby-leaf salad leaves, spinach and annual herbs all have a short shelf life. Sweetcorn loses half its sweetness within 12 hours of picking; peas lose a quarter.

Vegetables you buy in the shops have usually been picked at least a week before. Yet young, sweet and tender crops lose sugars rapidly; and many fruits are a shadow of their full richness if picked before they're ripe. It's these types of veg where growing your own wins every time.

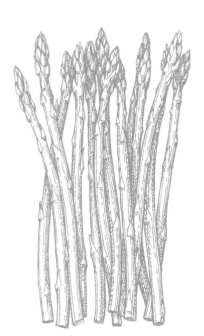

Every minute counts

Some fruit, like peaches and plums, must be picked just at the point of ripeness to enjoy their full sweetness. Asparagus spears also taste sublime when cut fresh to eat straightaway. And some veg are simply hard to find in the shops: heritage beefsteak tomatoes dripping with juice, tart cape gooseberries and fresh baby broad beans are all treats you only get to relish when you grow your own.

Asparagus,
Asparagus officinalis

Does how you feed and water make a difference to flavour?

SO YOU'RE CHOOSING VARIETIES CAREFULLY, **majoring on those with superior flavour; you're picking at the point of perfection; and you're eating directly after harvest. Is there anything else you can do to intensify flavour? What about watering and feeding?**

Flavour in fruit and veg is a complex soup of chemicals. Sugar – the energy the plant uses to grow – is the one we enjoy most, but there are other, more complex influences. The sulphurous taste of garlic, peppery capsaicin in chillies, and the spicy flavours in rocket or watercress are all natural pest defences. The mineral content of soil also matters: a potato grown on heavy, acidic clay has a subtly different flavour to the same variety grown in thin, alkaline chalk.

Feeding for flavour

Feeding your plants is all about maximizing their uptake of minerals found in your soil – but some nutrients are better for flavour than others. Nitrogen, for example, is fast food for plants: it makes plants grow quickly but sappy, with lower quantities of sugar, acids, magnesium and calcium – all of which contribute to flavour.

You'll get better results from a slower approach, adding organic matter to build your soil gradually into a more balanced, all-round blend of trace elements and minerals. If you're feeding in pots, more complex plant

tonics like liquid seaweed are better sources of micronutrients than feeds concentrated on one particular element such as potassium (which is found in tomato feeds).

Thirsty plants are tastier

Watering is also crucial to flavour: too much water dilutes sugars and other flavour chemicals. Less water also diverts a plant's energies to fruit, rather than leaves; it also encourages roots to dig deeper into the soil, bringing up minerals which in turn give complexity to flavours.

Cutting back on water by about half as fruits begin to ripen puts your plants in a mild state of drought stress. This won't harm the plant but will make a difference to the flavours. Chillies get spicier, while tomatoes and melons become sweeter. Sugar levels in root vegetables like carrots and beetroot almost double in drier conditions.

For leafy veg, though, the opposite is true. The peppery flavour in rocket and mustard goes from pleasantly spicy to eye-wateringly hot if they don't get enough water, while lettuce leaves will turn bitter. So watering controls the flavour – and you get to choose how spicy or sweet you'd like your salads.

The heat in chilli peppers is actually a pest defence and makes the plant unpalatable to many insects – but not to birds, which can't taste it.

Keeping rocket well watered ensures the peppery flavours stay within bearable limits and keeps the plant leafier for longer, too.

How your plants grow has as much effect on their eventual flavour as anything else. The chemicals that we taste as flavour are often a plant's response to other things entirely, from stress to pests to minerals in the soil. Water and feed carefully and you'll bring out these flavour compounds to the full.

How can I make sure there's something to pick from my veg garden every day of the year?

SUMMER IN BUSY VEGETABLE GARDENS is a time of overwhelming abundance, with so much to pick you hardly know where to start. But how do you make sure it doesn't all come to a shuddering full stop once cold weather hits?

Grow winter-lings like kale, sprouts, broccoli and leeks (above) off to one side in a 'nursery' bed until they're young plants, then transplant into gaps left by early summer harvests.

A winter veg garden is a gardener's paradise: you can pick your fill, yet the weeds have (largely) stopped growing and pests have gone to ground. Planning is the key to a well-stocked veg garden in the off season – and this starts the previous spring.

The mainstays of the winter veg garden (brassicas, leeks, parsnips and the like) are sown in spring, like other veg, but grow achingly slowly, taking almost a year to mature – so they miss the summer party and come into their own only once winter hits.

Each spring, plan your growing year like a relay race so winter harvests take over seamlessly as summer crops fade, with 'hungry gap' crops ready to take up the baton next spring.

Sow your main winter supplies in late spring (no earlier, or they'll mature too soon). Then follow up with

STORE-CUPBOARD STAPLES

These are veg you can have somewhere on the plot all year – giving you something to pick every day:

Chard White-stemmed varieties are hardier for winter picking.

Kale Sow thinner-leaved 'Red Russian' for summer leaves or hardier 'Dwarf Green Curled' for winter.

Lettuce Sow hardier winter varieties from late summer; lettuces sown in autumn overwinter as seedlings, bursting into life in time for picking through spring.

Parsley 'Moss Curled' parsley stays green all year round: sow regularly for a steady supply.

Purple sprouting broccoli Choose varieties that mature at different rates through winter and spring, then add summer-cropping to pick year round.

Kale, *Brassica oleracea* Acephala Group

extra sowings in midsummer of fast-growing crops such as dwarf French beans, beetroot and mangetout peas to keep the harvests coming throughout autumn, until the first frosts knock them down.

At the same time, sow winter salad supplies in pots under cover ready to plant outside in autumn. Winter lettuces, hardy Oriental leaves like mizuna, and annual herbs such as chervil, coriander and claytonia will stay green for most of the winter (cloches can help in bad weather).

Cater for the notorious early spring 'hungry gap' with store-cupboard staples (see above), plus the few crops at their best at this time of year – asparagus, spring cabbage and purple sprouting broccoli – and you'll have plenty of good things to eat until summer starts again.

Should I sow my seeds into pots or direct into the ground?

WHEN YOU COME TO SOW YOUR SEEDS, you're faced with a bewildering array of choices. You can sow into seedtrays, pots or modules, or just straight into the ground. So which method gives the best results?

The various methods of sowing have evolved to meet the needs of different types of seed – so match your sowing method to your seed variety and you can't go far wrong.

Where you can, sow direct as it's less work, and seedlings grow quicker when left undisturbed. Deep-rooted crops like parsnips and carrots don't always grow well in pots, so sowing direct is usually the only option.

Wait until the soil is properly warm (at least 10°C/50°F) before sowing: this is usually in mid- to late spring. Keep seeds damp while they're germinating and patrol daily at dusk looking for slugs.

In the chill of early spring – or when sowing the crops that slugs and mice like best (that's most of them, but particularly lettuce, courgettes, peas, beans and sweetcorn) – sowing into

DO I NEED A COLD FRAME?

Cold frames are essentially big wooden boxes with windows instead of lids. They make great stand-ins for greenhouses,

invaluable for keeping seedlings warm and sheltered; and if you do have a greenhouse, cold frames help 'harden off' seedlings, acclimatizing them to outdoor conditions. Wooden cold frame kits are inexpensive, but small: make your own from recycled pallet wood and old windows and you can have any size you like.

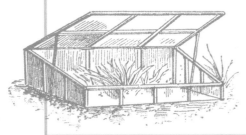

HOW TO SOW DIRECT

You can sow straight into mulches as long as they're fine enough: sieve rougher mulches first.

- Make a shallow drill (channel) no more than 1cm ($^1/_2$in) deep with the tip of a trowel.

- Water the bottom of the drill before you sow, so seeds go onto damp soil from the start.

- Sprinkle seed sparingly along the bottom – aim for about 1cm ($^1/_2$in) between each seed.

- Close the mulch back over the seeds until they're just covered.

pots keeps your babies warm, safe and easy to manage.

Sow finer seed you want lots of, like lettuces and leeks, in wooden seedtrays filled with good-quality seed compost. If you only need a few plants (tomatoes, for example), just sprinkle a pinch of seed into a 10cm (4in) clay pot. Larger seeds such as beans and sweetcorn go into cardboard loo roll inners. Keep warm, sheltered and well-watered and within 10–14 days you'll have a forest of seedlings.

You can repurpose just about any container for seed sowing. Punch holes in the bottom for drainage, fill with compost and sow.

Sowing direct into the ground is nature's way of doing things. But when the soil is still too cold for seeds to germinate or you're sowing slug caviar – like lettuces – it's a waste of time. In such cases, sowing seeds into pots may be more work, but you'll get better results.

How do I keep my containers watered?

CROPS IN CONTAINERS DEPEND ENTIRELY ON YOU **for their water supply. But pots are prone to drying out, especially in hot weather, hitting your harvest hard. So how can you keep your pots well-watered and your plants happy?**

Right from the start, do everything you can to help your container veg hold on to water. Loam-based composts – ideally home-made (see page 156) – hold on to more water than multipurpose composts; add a layer of well-rotted manure to the bottom for nutrients and to act as a sponge.

There's no need to add crocks or gravel for drainage: as long as your pot has drainage holes, that's enough. Terracotta pots are porous and dry out quicker, so it can help to line the pot with an old compost sack punched with holes for drainage.

Getting the watering right is the biggest challenge when growing veg in pots. Help your potted veg plot hold on to water by using water-retentive compost and lining containers before planting. Water daily in dry weather (and more often in heatwaves) or use self-watering pots and automatic watering systems to do the job for you.

Watering wisdom

Water early in the morning or in the evening so you don't lose water to evaporation, and really soak your pots each time. Test with your finger to make sure the water has reached the middle of the pot; if it's still dry at the centre, standing the pot in water almost to the rim for an hour helps rehydrate it fully.

Automated watering systems on timers keep pots watered more steadily, but they do need monitoring for the best results: adjust the timing to water more often in hot weather and check drippers occasionally to make sure they aren't blocked. Self-watering pots are more straightforward to use: just keep the reservoir topped up and then plants can choose for themselves how much water they need, for weeks at a time.

MAKE A SELF-WATERING POT

• Slot two buckets one inside the other, so there's a gap beneath for a reservoir.

• Cut a hole in the bottom of the top bucket and slot in a yoghurt pot, punched with 1cm ($^1/2$in) holes and then packed tightly with potting some compost.

• Next find a pipe 5cm (2in) wide and cut another hole in the bucket to slot this through. The top should stick up above the upper bucket; cut the bottom to 45 degrees to allow water through more easily.

• Finally, drill a 1cm ($^1/2$in) hole through the side of the lower bucket just below where the topmost bucket sits, to act as an overflow drain.

• Fill the top bucket with compost and plant; water in normally, then fill the reservoir (you'll know it's full when water runs out of the overflow hole). Keep topped up and your plants will water themselves.

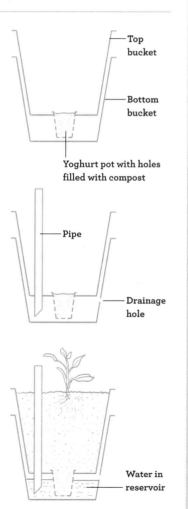

Top bucket

Bottom bucket

Yoghurt pot with holes filled with compost

Pipe

Drainage hole

Water in reservoir

It's stopped raining! What should I do?

CLIMATE CHANGE IS BRINGING INCREASINGLY EXTREME WEATHER, from torrential rain and devastating storms to exceptionally long periods of drought – all of which make growing your own food more challenging. So how do you keep your crops growing well when the rain has stopped?

Drought defence starts with the soil. Organic matter holds water within the soil like a sponge – so mulch generously, always onto damp soil and without digging it in, as turning soil helps moisture evaporate.

Some crops cope with drought better than others. Leafy salads and spinach, podding or fruiting crops, and shallow-rooted crops like peas really suffer, so prioritize these, as well as newly sown seeds and young plants. In extremis, take a break from growing drought-sensitive crops in high summer, starting again with sowings in early autumn. Plant early peas in spring to produce a crop before a drought, then freeze the surplus to keep you going until the weather cools.

Plants are most in need of water when they're fruiting, so concentrate supplies on these to safeguard your harvest.

For most crops, drought is a crisis and they respond by conserving resources. Often that means tougher, bitter-tasting leaves, slower growth, less fruit and smaller roots – all disastrous for your end-of-season harvest. Drought-proof your soil, major on drought-tolerant crops and conserve your own water supplies to give your veg garden the best chance of pulling through.

Crops for dry gardens

Crops with succulent midribs like chard (an excellent drought-tolerant spinach substitute), deep-rooted veg such as carrots and parsnips, and plants adapted to harsh, dry climates like Mediterranean herbs and globe artichokes will soldier on through water shortages.

It also helps if you can store some of the rain from the winter to see you through summer shortages. Harvest rainwater from the roof of your house, sheds or greenhouses and collect in tanks as large as you have room for: you can link several water butts together with connection kits. If you don't have buildings, freestanding rain saucers – like upside-down umbrellas – catch rain and feed it into a storage tank beneath.

Globe artichoke,
Cynara cardunculus
Scolymus Group

DROUGHT GARDENING STRATEGIES

Soaker hoses
Lay porous soaker hoses in S bends through your crops, cover with shallow mulch and connect to a water supply via a conventional hose to deliver water without any wastage.

Clay pot watering
Sink plant pots into the ground to the rim alongside thirsty plants like squash and tomatoes, and water into the top: they'll deliver moisture gradually right into the root zone.

Shade tunnels
Give leafy veg like lettuces and spinach the shade they crave with a cover made of calico or muslin, helping slow water evaporation from both soil and plants.

Clay pot

What's so bad about peat?

FOR MORE THAN 60 YEARS, gardeners around the world have relied heavily on peat in potting composts and to raise plants for sale. But moves are now afoot to get peat out of horticulture; so what's so bad about it?

HOW TO GARDEN WITHOUT PEAT

- **Buy peat-free compost** If it doesn't say 'peat-free' on the bag, it probably contains peat. 'Organic', 'sustainable' or 'eco-friendly' do not mean peat-free.

- **Be fussy about your brand** There are now excellent peat-free brands – some outperform peat-based composts in trials. Stick to these and don't be tempted by cheap offers.

- **Make your own 'peat'** Make leafmould (see page 112) or rot down wood chip for a couple of years for peat substitutes to use in home-made potting mixes.

There's nothing bad about peat itself: it's a remarkable material, formed over thousands of years as organic plant material decays in the damp of a peat bog. But digging it up to use in gardening releases the carbon it contains, oxidizing it to form carbon dioxide and contributing to climate change. It's also unnecessary, as there are perfectly good alternatives.

Peat bogs may only cover three percent of the world's surface, but they're one of our most efficient carbon sinks – better at locking up carbon than any other ecosystem, including rainforests. They're also unique ecosystems full of rare flowers and

The peat extracted commercially from a bog in a single year will have taken around ten thousand years to form.

BUYING PLANTS WITHOUT THE PEAT

When you're buying a ready-grown plant, whether it's a plug plant or in a pot, it's almost certainly been grown in peat-based compost.

Fruit trees and bushes are available bare-root, dug up from the field in winter while still dormant. You can buy strawberries, berry fruit, trees, raspberry canes and rhubarb crowns bare-root, online or in garden centres from mid-autumn to early spring.

You may be able to find peat-free vegetable plug plants in garden centres and you can also buy high-quality, peat-free plug plants online or via mail order. If these are organic, you'll also know that they haven't been treated with any pesticides.

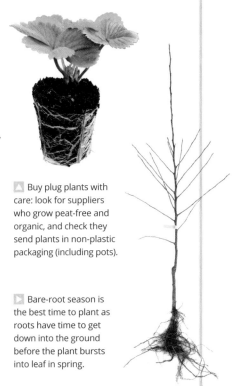

Buy plug plants with care: look for suppliers who grow peat-free and organic, and check they send plants in non-plastic packaging (including pots).

Bare-root season is the best time to plant as roots have time to get down into the ground before the plant bursts into leaf in spring.

insects, as well as absorbing rainwater to prevent flooding and acting like a filter to clean our drinking water.

Draining peat bogs and digging them up to extract the peat they contain is turning our best carbon sinks into net carbon emitters. And because peat forms so slowly, it's a one-way street. Once we've dug the peat up, it won't regenerate for another ten thousand years.

There's simply no need to use peat in this way. There are excellent alternatives to peat, just as moisture-retentive, lightweight and fine-textured, which do just as good a job at raising your plants. Peat-free potting composts based on these materials (mainly wood fibre, composted bark, coir and municipal green waste) are now widely available to the home gardener.

What's the best way to deal with garden waste?

YOU DON'T HAVE TO GARDEN FOR LONG to build up a pile of garden waste – weeds, prunings and spent plants accumulate as you sow, plant and tend your veg. But how can you deal with it all in a way that's also planet-friendly?

Every plant in the garden, from the tiniest weed to the biggest tree, is full of carbon-rich organic matter, part of the great cycle of life that plays out in your garden. When you weed, or prune, or tidy you take this away – and it's up to you to put it back.

Keep your garden waste inside your gate and you can feed your soil and your plants as well as boost your soil's ecosystem. Along the way, you can create habitats for wildlife and make your own building materials: wood chip made from shredded prunings makes a wonderful material for garden paths. And you'll never have to spend an afternoon at your local recycling depot again.

There's an easy way to make your garden waste disappear: just start seeing it as an extra harvest. Green waste is a fantastic resource: use it to make compost, increase biodiversity and even build garden paths. You'll want to hang on to every scrap.

Green 'waste' is full of nitrogen and other essential plant nutrients, as well as carbon; return it to the ground and it will feed your plants.

Stag beetle larvae feed mainly on decaying wood for up to seven years before emerging as an adult beetle up to 7.5cm (3in) long.

You can add diseased plant waste to your compost heap: rain-borne fungal disease such as mildew, rust and late blight don't survive composting. But separate out plants affected by soil-borne diseases like clubroot or verticillium wilt and take them to your council recycling centre instead.

Make a dead hedge

Don't be put off by the name: dead hedges are full of life. Make one in an out-of-the-way spot at the back of your garden and it'll take all your woody waste and provide a home for every kind of wildlife, from hedgehogs to stag beetles.

Drive parallel staggered rows of fence posts into the ground, about 1m (3ft) apart. Then stack your woody waste inside, starting with longer branches at the outside to hold everything in place. As the material rots, returning the carbon it contains to the earth, the level will fall, allowing you to top up with more waste.

WASTE PROCESSING

You can put every scrap of green waste to good use, from the smallest weed to the thickest tree trunk.

Weeds and other green waste
Add annual weeds and perennial top growth straight to the compost heap: drown perennial weed roots in water before adding them too (for details, see page 119).

Fibrous stems and prunings up to 5cm (2in)
Shred with an electric garden shredder and add to the compost or use (bulked up with wood chippings from local tree surgeons) to make garden paths.

Branches thicker than 5cm (2in)
Cut into 30cm (12in) lengths and stack into logpiles to return the carbon to the earth, while providing a home for frogs, toads and ground beetles.

Is it worth making my own potting compost?

VEG GROWERS GET THROUGH A LOT OF POTTING COMPOST what with all that sowing, pricking out and potting on. But bought compost is expensive and arrives in plastic compost sacks – so can you avoid the plastic and save money by making your own?

You've probably already got most materials for making potting mixes in your garden. The three main ingredients are loam (another name for garden soil), garden compost from your compost heap, and leafmould (see page 112) or wood chip mulch that's been rotted for at least two years.

You can also add organic fertilizers, sharp sand for extra drainage, and special ingredients like composted bracken for ericaceous (acidic) potting compost, ideal for acid-loving

Making your own potting mixes is something of a lost art. Once every keen gardener had their favourite, jealously guarded recipes, but nowadays we've fallen out of the habit. It's a shame, as home-made potting mixes are not only cheaper and better for the planet – they're often better for your plants.

blueberries. The beauty of making your own is that you can tweak your recipes, like baking a cake, until you get the blend just right. And as it's based on the soil your plants will eventually be growing in, they won't have much adjustment to make when you plant them out in the garden.

**Bracken,
*Pteridium
aquilinum***

**Blueberry,
*Vaccinium
corymbosum***

POTTING COMPOSTS FOR EVERY PURPOSE

Sowing seeds
A low-nutrient mix is ideal for growing seed. Sow straight into plain, sieved, two-year-old leafmould, or for a mix that supports seedlings a little longer, blend equal parts of garden soil, leafmould and sharp sand.

Taking cuttings
You need a richer mix with sharper drainage. One part garden topsoil and one part home-made compost provide the bulk, then add two parts of sharp sand.

Potting on
You want the equivalent of full-strength, loam-based multipurpose compost. Mix three parts home-made compost, two parts garden soil and one part leafmould, then add slow-release feed – about one trowelful of seaweed meal to a wheelbarrow full of potting mix.

Make as much or as little as you want, and match the compost you're making to the purpose you want it for.

Garden compost versus potting compost
The compost that you buy in a plastic bag from the local garden centre is potting compost – a blend of several ingredients such as loam, wood fibre, green waste and composted bark, all carefully balanced to help your plants grow well. Garden compost, however, is just one ingredient, made by recycling green waste, kitchen scraps and other organic matter in a compost heap (see page 132). Garden compost

You can tailor potting compost mixes to suit the needs of the plants you are intending to grow in them.

is great for improving your soil, but plants will not grow successfully in it unless you add some other ingredients, like topsoil, to turn it into a suitable potting compost.

Chapter **4**

What's Eating
My Crops?

How can I climate-proof my plot?

As CLIMATE CHANGE TAKES HOLD, it seems each year brings new challenges for us and our plants, from month-long spring frosts to endless droughts or biblical downpours. So what can we do to protect the veg plot and keep on growing?

Climate-proofing your plot is all about softening the extremes of cold, heat and flood to help plants cope. You can't do much about the weather, but there's plenty you can do to protect your crops. Any measure you take to climate-proof your plot builds resilience in the wider environment.

Knowing when to sow is tricky when spring might bring anything from a heatwave to frost – so make two or three sowings, a month apart. Then if one doesn't make it, there's another to replace it.

Climate change means new, exotic pests are surviving outside their normal range and existing pests emerge early. So use a barrage of tactics. Patrol plants for pests all year round, keep greenhouses tidy to leave pests no place to hide and recruit natural predators to help keep them under control.

Gardens as carbon sinks

Just by growing plants you're helping soften the extremes brought about by climate change. Well-cultivated soil helps absorb excess rainfall and all plants remove carbon dioxide from the atmosphere – helping tackle the causes of climate change, too.

Drought-tolerant, high-yielding and relatively pest-free crops like kale weather extreme climate events better than most.

Climate change isn't all bad news for veg growers: rising temperatures are giving us a much longer season most years. But it's also bringing very unpredictable extreme weather events, which can wreck your hard work overnight. Take steps to buffer your plot against the worst, and you should still be able to gather a good harvest.

CLIMATE-PROOFING STRATEGIES

Shelter from the storm

Climate change whips winds into storm-force gales, so plant hedges to filter the worst of these. Use tall clumps of Jerusalem artichokes or blackcurrants to shelter lower-growing crops and stake Brussels sprouts, kale and purple sprouting broccoli firmly, so they don't blow over.

Managing water

In a climate-changed garden you're likely to have far too much water in winter and nowhere near enough in summer. So manage your supply by installing extra water tanks to store rainwater for later. Ponds and rain gardens help absorb excess rainwater, while keeping soil mulched with organic matter helps cushion your plants through both droughts and floods.

Blackcurrant,
Ribes nigrum

Link water butts together using connector kits to boost your rainwater storage capacity.

Resilient plants

In an unpredictable climate you're likely to have more crop failures, so grow a wide selection of crops to ensure at least some will thrive whatever conditions you get. Apples, blackcurrants, strawberries and garlic can fail to crop after mild winters, so look for low chill requirement varieties such as apple 'Dorsett Golden' and strawberry 'Camarosa'.

Q Can I eat my weeds?

WEEDS GROW SO SUCCESSFULLY it's hard not to be a little envious. After all, if you could get your crops to grow that easily, growing your own food would be a doddle. Now there's an idea: are there any weeds you can eat?

A Weeds get a bad press, but they're plants just like any other and often really useful to have in the garden. Some are also edible, so you can forage a never-ending supply of tasty and unusual greens from plants you'd otherwise be throwing on the compost heap.

Most weeds are actually nectar-rich wildflowers, adored by bees – think cow parsley, daisies and buttercups. Others feed your crops: clover fixes nitrogen, while dandelion roots draw minerals from deep underground. And if that's not enough reason to love your weeds – many can feed you, too.

TASTY WEEDS

Chickweed, *Stellaria media*

Dandelion If you like the mildly bitter taste of chicory, you'll enjoy dandelion leaves. Cover crowns with black pots to blanch and sweeten young leaves.

Nettles Fresh young nettle tips picked (with gloves on) in spring taste a little like kale and make a nourishing soup; you can brew a passable beer from them too!

Chickweed This ubiquitous low-growing annual is easily identified by its starry white flowers: snip shoot tips as required for lettuce-like salad greens.

Q Why have my strawberries suddenly wilted?

JUST OCCASIONALLY IN THE VEG PLOT, DISASTER STRIKES without warning. You come out to do the watering as usual and your strawberries – the picture of health the day before – are wilting and sad. What's gone wrong?

Firstly, look for other symptoms. Notches chewed from leaf edges are evidence of adult weevils; tip the plants out of the pot, or dig them up, and if you find small, C-shaped, creamy maggots devouring the roots, you've caught the culprit red-handed.

You might still save the plants: clean the roots in water, then pot up in fresh compost and hopefully the roots will regrow. Avoid reinfestation by watering with nematodes (see page 186) from midsummer to autumn when vine weevils are most active.

A Diagnosing what's wrong with your crops is a process of elimination, starting with the most likely cause and working backwards. In this case, vine weevils are the prime suspect. They're very common and strawberries are a favourite target. Sudden wilting is among the first signs that your plants are under attack.

OTHER CAUSES OF SUDDEN WILTING

Too little or too much water Confusingly, both drought and waterlogging cause the same symptoms: find out which it is and then adjust your watering regime accordingly.

Frost damage Sudden frosts can cause wilting: shoots may look alarmingly withered but the plant usually recovers.

Verticillium wilt Nasty, soil-borne fungal disease affecting tomatoes, strawberries and other veg. There's no cure, so if confirmed (look for tell-tale brown rings inside the stem), you'll have to switch to container growing instead.

Verticillium wilt

Can anything stop blight?

IT STARTS IN LATE SUMMER with brown blotches on potato or tomato leaves: within a fortnight you're salvaging what's left of your crop from a mess of rotting stems. Blight is an annual scourge for most veg growers – so can anything stop it?

◀ Late blight is caused by a rampant fungus-like organism, *Phytophthora infestans*, and affects only potatoes and tomatoes.

Blight strikes when very specific conditions are met: two consecutive days at 10°C (50°F) with at least six hours in each day when relative humidity is above 90 percent, known as the Hutton Criteria. In the UK, you can get alerts letting you know when blight is a real risk in your area (blightwatch.co.uk).

When blight hits potatoes and tomatoes, it's devastating. Pick off affected leaves to slow the spread, and once potato stems turn brown cut away top growth to save the tubers. But it is possible to fend off blight before things get that bad: grow under glass, stick to early potatoes or choose blight-resistant varieties from the start.

Avoiding blight

Mostly, blight hits the Goldilocks spot, when everything is just right, from midsummer. Early and second early potatoes harvested before then largely escape unscathed, so if you stick to these rather than blight-prone maincrops you'll still dig up a full harvest.

Protect tomatoes by growing them in a greenhouse. Blight needs damp foliage to land on and reproduce, so if you can keep the leaves dry, your tomatoes will be safe. Always water the base of the plant to avoid splashing leaves and close windows and doors on rainy days.

Soldiering on through

But even in very blight-prone areas like warm, damp southwest Britain it's still possible to grow tomatoes and maincrop potatoes outdoors if you choose blight-resistant varieties. These are modern strains bred to soldier on through onslaughts of blight: some are still affected, but mildly, while others are able to stand tall and healthy while lesser varieties collapse into a soggy mess. Grow these and you should have a trouble-free year – blight or no blight. However, blight is notoriously good at mutating, so keep an eye out for any new developments and be ready to switch to updated varieties as they're released to stay one step ahead.

▼ Tomatoes inside greenhouses can still get blight, but only if you let the rain in – so close windows and doors on rainy summer days.

BLIGHT-RESISTANT VARIETIES

Potatoes

'Sarpo Mira' One of the 'Sarpo' family, along with 'Axona' and 'Shona', all with superb blight resistance.

'Alouette' Red-skinned, waxy salad potato: both foliage and tubers are resistant to blight.

'Carolus' Floury maincrop with large tubers that keep well: both foliage and tubers are blight resistant.

Tomatoes

'Mountain Magic' One of the best-flavoured, most blight-resistant tomatoes with masses of smallish fruits.

'Oh Happy Day' Beefsteak-style tomatoes with an exceptional flavour and good blight resistance.

'Losetto' Waterfalls of cherry tomatoes on compact plants ideal for containers or even hanging baskets.

What crops will be a feast for me and for wildlife?

VEG GROWERS HAVE LONG HAD A LOVE-HATE RELATIONSHIP with wildlife: after all, many of the birds and bugs that visit our plots enjoy eating our crops as much as we do. Can you grow veg and boost biodiversity without losing your harvest?

Wildlife-friendly gardens come with built-in pest control. Make your plot inviting for birds, ladybirds, hedgehogs and ground beetles and they quickly get to work tucking into your resident aphids, caterpillars and slugs.

Letting nature take charge of your pest control can take some getting used to. Bear in mind that pesticide spray – synthetic or organic – kills both pests and beneficial insects, potentially making your problem worse if pests come back before their predators do. In a wildlife-friendly veg garden there's a low-level pest presence all the time, so you do have to expect some cosmetic damage. It

When pests get out of hand, it's not because there's too much wildlife in your garden: it's because there's too little. A healthy veg plot is full of life, with a vibrant ecosystem where pest populations are kept in check by the predators who eat them. Grow crops to encourage a rich biodiversity and everyone feasts.

should stay at a level you can tolerate, though, as populations shouldn't get out of control enough to ruin your crops.

Target pest protection
That said, you'll need to keep the wildlife off some crops while your harvest is at its peak or risk losing the lot. Cover berry bushes with mesh cages as fruits start to colour and grow brassicas under insect-proof mesh. But target pest protection only when and where it's needed, and let the wildlife back in as soon as you finish picking.

▲ A ladybird can eat thousands of aphids in its lifetime: they're at their most voracious while in their spiky, black-and-yellow larval stage.

WILDLIFE-FRIENDLY FOOD

Courgette,
Cucurbita pepo

Grow flowering crops

Climbing beans, courgettes, pumpkins and peas are magnets for bees when in flower – and as they pollinate their blooms, they help plants set a bigger crop.

Add edible flowers

Nasturtiums, pot marigolds (*Calendula*) and violets provide valuable nectar for pollinating insects, and you can steal some flowers for your salads, too.

Nasturtium,
*Tropaeolum
majus*

Tuck in a few herbs

Pop rosemary, thyme, chives and sage into odd corners and let them flower for the bees; clip evergreen bay into dense balls where sparrows can nest and hedgehogs can hide.

Let your crops flower

Leave a few carrots, parsnips and leeks in the ground into their second year and they'll burst into nectar-rich flowers – followed by seeds you can save for next year's crop.

Apple,
Malus domestica

Grow fruit

Spring blossom on fruit trees is an important early source of nectar; leave a share of your berries at the end of your harvest so birds can feast too.

How can I get rid of slugs?

SLUGS ARE THE GARDENER'S NUMBER ONE ENEMY. They raze
newly emerged seedlings to the ground, reduce lettuce leaves to
tatters and ravage previously pristine potato tubers. So what can
you do to get them out of your garden?

ANTI-SLUG STRATEGIES

Night patrols
Every evening at dusk, especially after rain, go on a slug safari around
your most vulnerable crops, picking off any you see.

Bran barriers
The only effective barrier as bran swells up in rain rather than washing
away; heap in a ring around individual plants at risk, like courgettes.

Swimming pools
Slugs can swim, but don't like to – so stand containers in a wide saucer
of water, lifted on pot feet so they don't get waterlogged, and slugs
should go elsewhere.

Nematodes
These naturally occurring microscopic creatures prey on slugs living
underground and are available as a biological control, watered on to
beds of vulnerable crops from late spring (see page 186).

Ferric phosphate pellets
These slug pellets are approved for organic growing and are effective,
but use very sparingly and only as a last resort as there is some
evidence they can harm earthworms.

◁ There are about 40 species of
slug in the UK, but only nine of them
do any damage to plants.

It may be hard to love a slug, but they're actually helping your garden. Most species eat mainly decomposing plants, helping turn them into compost. They also clear away dead animals and excrement, and underpin biodiversity as a plentiful food for all sorts of creatures, from birds to ground beetles.

The trouble is, slugs insist on eating the food you want to eat too. There are some crops they don't like: parsnips, peppery leaves like nasturtiums, rocket and mustard, Mediterranean herbs, and for some reason red-leaved lettuces. But most green leaves are fair game.

Protect vulnerable crops

Concentrate your efforts on plants that are most severely affected by slug attack: seedlings, tender-leaved, succulent plants like lettuces, and leafy veg such as spinach and cabbages. Slugs prefer young growth and can devastate newly emerging seedlings in the open garden. So rather than sowing direct, sow into pots. Keep seedlings on shelves, where they're harder for slugs to reach, and inspect underneath and between pots daily, picking off any slugs you find. Once they're sturdy youngsters, you can plant them safely outside as they're less attractive to slugs and able to withstand a little damage.

SLUG CATCHERS

Place wooden planks, bricks, roof tiles or upside-down, hollowed-out grapefruit halves near vulnerable plants in the veg patch and slugs and snails will congregate beneath.

Slugs love the cool, damp conditions under planks, roof tiles and bricks.

The average British garden is home to a staggering 20,000 slugs. So you may as well accept you'll never be rid of them altogether – and that's a good thing, as slugs and snails play a crucial role in garden ecosystems. Instead, work around them, defending vulnerable crops but letting predators deal with the rest.

Should I spray caterpillars and aphids?

APHIDS AND CATERPILLARS CAN BE DEVASTATING.
Infestations of sap-sucking aphids weaken plants and hit your
harvest, while caterpillars can reduce healthy leaves to skeletons.
So what should you do when you find your plants under attack?
Should you reach for the spray bottle?

Aphids (greenfly and blackfly)
multiply with eye-watering speed
– they're born already pregnant and
colonies can triple every day. Each
small cabbage white butterfly lays up
to 100 eggs in a cluster: if they all
develop into full-sized caterpillars,
they'll easily strip a cabbage bare.
Once colonies get that big the damage
to your plants becomes noticeable, and
they are almost impossible to control.
You may limit the damage, but you'll

CONTROLLING CATERPILLARS

• Patrol brassicas (cabbages, sprouts, kale and
broccoli, but also turnips, swedes and
nasturtiums), turning leaves over to look
for clutches of tiny eggs.

• Pick off caterpillars by hand – though
once caterpillars hatch you're unlikely to
avoid damage.

• Once caterpillars are present, there's a
spray-on biological control that works on
contact – apply during cool, damp weather.

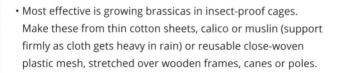

Cabbage white butterfly eggs on a broccoli leaf

• Most effective is growing brassicas in insect-proof cages.
Make these from thin cotton sheets, calico or muslin (support
firmly as cloth gets heavy in rain) or reusable close-woven
plastic mesh, stretched over wooden frames, canes or poles.

CONTROLLING APHIDS

- Plants tolerate a small numbers of aphids, so don't worry about getting rid of them all; but patrol daily, inspecting shoot tips and leaves so you know when populations start to build.

- Squashing small infestations between finger and thumb stops them getting out of control.

- Using the garden hose on jet setting to hose aphids off plants daily until the outbreak retreats is also very effective.

- In greenhouses, release parasitoid wasps as a biological control to keep outbreaks in check.

Colemani wasp,
Aphidius colemani

- Pinching out broad bean plant tips in early summer, after they've set their pods, removes the part of the plant blackfly like best – so they'll go elsewhere.

never get back the harvest you would have had if you hadn't let things get out of hand.

A healthy garden ecosystem will do much to keep both aphids and caterpillars under control, as almost every creature in your garden enjoys snacking on aphids – from ladybirds, lacewings, hoverflies, earwigs and wasps to sparrows. Caterpillars have fewer predators but they include hedgehogs, some birds and shrews.

When caterpillars and aphids multiply to the point where they're doing serious damage, it's an emergency situation and organic sprays can be the 999 service you need. But if you get to this stage, really it's too late: far better to prevent the situation getting this bad in the first place.

House sparrow,
Passer domesticus

Do bug hotels help in a vegetable garden?

BUG HOTELS ARE GREAT FUN and make a really quirky feature in the garden. They're a must-have for wildlife gardens, but can they be useful in the veg garden too? Don't they just provide a handy haven for pests?

WHO LIVES WHERE?

Think about which creatures you'd like to host in your hotel – and choose your materials accordingly. Make sure all materials are natural and untreated, and avoid plastic which encourages damp and mould.

Mason bee, *Osmia xanthomelana*

Bug hotels in full sun:

Solitary bees, including mason bees and leafcutter bees, need small tubes, 2–10mm (¼in) in diameter. Bundle together 10cm (4in) lengths of hollow plant stems or bamboo canes, or drill holes of different diameters deep into a block of untreated wood.

Ladybirds and lacewings colonize dry leaves, twigs and hollow plant stems, and creep into rolled-up corrugated cardboard.

Bug hotels in damp, shady spots:

Beetles, centipedes and millipedes – all of which guzzle slug eggs – enjoy damp logs and loose bark.

Frogs and toads like stones and clay roof tiles, ideally in the middle of the hotel where it's cool but frost-free – perfect for hibernating.

Common toad, *Bufo bufo*

Lacewing
house

The best bug hotels are home-made, as you can custom-design the living accommodation to make sure it's suitable for the creatures you most want to house. You can also leave larger cavities at the bottom for bigger creatures like hedgehogs. Two or three smaller bug hotels are better than one enormous one, as it's easier to create the different environments each wild creature needs.

HOW TO BUILD A BUG HOTEL

• Lay bricks on level ground in an H-shape.

• Rest three or four wooden pallets on top: cut them in half or quarters for smaller hotels.

• Cut away the slats in one corner to make space for a hedgehog house.

• Fill each gap with a different material.

• Finish off with a waterproof roof made from old tiles or secondhand roofing felt.

Looking after your bug hotel

Just like real hotels, bug hotels need a clean from time to time to keep their residents happy. Solitary bees can be attacked by parasitic wasps and flies, and mouldy, decaying materials cause disease.

In late spring, after eggs have hatched, inspect nesting tubes for dead cells. Clean holes with a pipe cleaner, or remove and replace hollow canes. Replace the straw and twigs. Every two years, remove and replace drilled wood blocks.

Some pests – mainly slugs and snails – do make themselves at home in bug hotels. But they're living dangerously, as their neighbours – like toads, hedgehogs and ladybirds – are almost all natural predators and will help to protect your crops. Bug hotels also house solitary bees, lacewings and other pollinating insects, boosting your harvest. Every veg plot should have one.

Are some vegetables immune to disease?

SOME CROPS ARE EASY TO GROW and produce a great crop without ever getting sick. Others need coaxing along every step of the way and fall prey to every ailment in the book. So are some vegetables naturally immune to disease?

Just like people, some veg have naturally robust constitutions. Others are a little more frail, needing cosseting to get them to give their best. That's not to say you can't grow them, as there are often varieties bred to resist certain diseases: stick to these and you'll make your veg-growing life a lot easier.

Disease-resistant veg help you grow more sustainably, as you won't have to use sprays to protect them, or extra feed and water to nurse them back to health. They tend to be more productive for less effort, largely looking after themselves.

Most diseases attack a particular type of crop. The nasty fungal disease clubroot devastates all kinds of brassicas (kale, interestingly, is often less badly affected), while onion white rot targets alliums – onions, garlic

BOMB-PROOF VEG

- Runner beans

- Climbing French beans

- Chard

- Kale

- Asparagus

- Mediterranean herbs

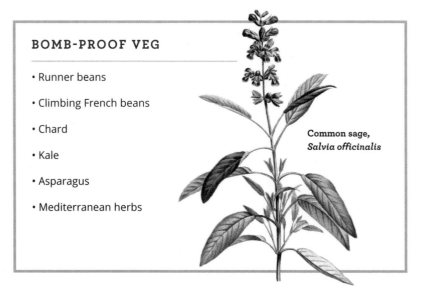

Common sage,
Salvia officinalis

◁ Stunted growth, wilting foliage (often tinted purple) and lumpy, misshapen roots are tell-tale signs of clubroot.

and leeks. Some veg families simply don't suffer much disease, including the more vigorous types of legume, resilient perennials like asparagus, and less highly bred crops, like herbs.

Breeding in disease resistance

Even where disease is a real risk, disease-resistant varieties allow you to grow susceptible veg even in affected areas. Blight-resistant tomatoes like 'Losetto', for example, grow happily outdoors, even in warm, damp areas like the southwest of England where blight spores in rain are a fact of life (see page 164).

However, immunity from disease doesn't always last. Least stable are F1 varieties, bred 'vertically' from a very limited gene pool: they include valuable disease-resistant varieties such as blight-resistant tomatoes and clubroot-resistant brassicas, but they're vulnerable to diseases mutating. Open-pollinated varieties,

CREATE YOUR OWN DISEASE-RESISTANT VARIETY

If you have an outbreak of disease on the plot, but some plants hold out longer than others, you have the building blocks for your own disease-resistant variety.

Mark the resistant plants with coloured wool and collect their seeds (see page 204). The following year, sow the second generation and observe how they deal with infection, saving seed only from plants that show the same resistance. After a few generations, you'll have a home-bred variety with at least some natural ability to shrug off infection.

bred 'horizontally' via natural selection over generations, have broader genetic foundations, so their resistance to disease is less likely to break down over time. Even better, you can save seed from these varieties (unlike F1 strains), so their offspring will be disease resistant, too.

Why have I got so many weeds?

YOU SPEND HOURS ON YOUR HANDS AND KNEES painstakingly pulling out weeds so they don't compete with your crops for nutrients and water. Then a week later they're back, launching another veg bed invasion. So why are there so many?

Weeds are nature's opportunists. Every time you leave soil bare, turn seeds to the light or fragment perennial roots they seize the chance to create new colonies. Close off these toeholds where weeds can take root and you should find your endless hours of weeding dwindle almost to nothing.

The top 10cm (4in) of your soil is one giant seed packet, filled with thousands of seeds of dozens of different plants – and most of them are annual weeds. When conditions are just right, they start growing enthusiastically, and those conditions are usually created by the gardener.

Put away the fork

Whenever you dig you're turning your soil's seed bank to the light, triggering germination. Stop digging and blanket the soil with mulch instead, and you bury the seeds beneath 5–8cm (2–3in) of organic matter, excluding light and burying them deep down where they can't cause trouble.

You do still get blow-ins germinating on top of the mulch, but it's an easy job to hoe them off, cutting away top growth just below the soil's surface, or simply pull them out of the loose mulch with your fingers.

Allow a few less competitive weeds, like herb robert, cow parsley and lawn

Weeds compete with your crops for light, food and water, so keep them under control – but leave a few to grow and help local pollinators.

daisies: they're free nectar to entice pollinating insects nearer to your crops and help distract pests too.

Persistent offenders

Hoeing also works well for perennial weeds. Bindweed and marestail regenerate from roots as deep as 2–5m (6½–16ft) below ground, so it's pointless to try digging them out. And many perennial weeds, including couch grass and ground elder, resprout from each end of a broken root, so digging can actually double your problem.

Bindweed,
Calystegia sepium

Cow parsley,
Anthriscus sylvestris

Perennial weeds are only plants, and they can't survive if they are unable to photosynthesize. So hoeing off or pulling out emerging shoots at least once a week steadily weakens them over time, even eliminating them altogether if you can keep it up for two or three years.

Cardboard to the rescue

Another option is to cover empty veg beds with thick cardboard. Make sure there are no gaps and dampen the cardboard, treading it down so it's flat to the soil. Then mulch thickly on top (10–15cm/4–6in deep) and plant or sow into the mulch. This gives you a year of weed-free growing before the perennial weeds break through the cardboard; simply repeat the process for the following year.

What's eating my veg?

SOMETHING'S BEEN TUCKING INTO YOUR VEG – but what?
One chewed leaf may look much like another, yet it's crucial to find
out who the culprit is so you know what to do about it. So how do you
know who has been eating your veg?

The right diagnosis is crucial
when you're trying to work out
what's ailing your crops. It's
easy to make mistakes and end
up treating the wrong problem.
Inspect your damaged plants
closely and gather as many
clues as you can before
deciding what the issue is.

The first thing to look for is
the pest itself. They'll often
congregate on shoot tips, or under
leaves, so look there first. Sometimes
it's obvious: caterpillars are hard to
miss. But red spider mite are tiny,
often no more than pale yellow specks
– so a magnifying glass can help.

Spotting sap-suckers

Sap-sucking insects don't make
visible holes, but they do cause shoot
tips to shrivel; leaves often become
mottled and turn a sickly yellow, too.
Sometimes there's black sooty mould
on lower leaves, growing on the
sweet honeydew excreted by the
insects above.

If the pest isn't physically
present, you can still narrow down
the possibilities. Some pests are
specific to a certain crop: so if
something is eating asparagus foliage,
it's almost certainly asparagus beetle,
while skeletonized gooseberry leaves
are likely to be gooseberry sawfly
larvae at work.

Gooseberry sawfly,
Nematus ribesii

KNOW YOUR HOLES

Pests have very distinctive ways of feeding, leaving a different type of damage like a signature on the leaf. So it's sometimes possible to identify your prime suspect just by looking at the holes it has made.

Flea beetles make small round holes in radish leaves.

Tiny round 'shot holes' peppering the leaves of young brassicas are the work of flea beetles: grow under mesh from the start to prevent them reaching your crops.

Ragged holes with slime trails mostly in the centre of leaves, but also at outer edges, are a giveaway that slugs have found your crops: patrol at dusk and pick off any you find.

Ragged holes without slime sometimes in leaf centres but mostly chewed from the edges are caused by cabbage white caterpillars: go over your plants daily, picking them off.

Cabbage white butterfly caterpillars eat irregular holes in brassica leaves.

Big chunks of leaf torn away leaving skeletonized leaves are all that's left after a visit from pigeons. Grow brassicas under mesh to keep them off.

Whole plants eaten down to a nub are signs you've had a visit from rabbits or deer, able to cause wholesale damage and ruin your crops overnight. Fencing is the only way to keep them out.

Pigeons tear great chunks out of cabbages.

How can I harvest herbs and let the bees enjoy their flowers?

HERB FLOWERS ARE SO RICH IN NECTAR they've hardly opened before they're buzzing with bees and hoverflies. But once herbs start flowering, they stop producing leaves – so how can you harvest your crops and help pollinating insects?

Herbs like thyme, sage, basil and oregano are best picked regularly to stimulate lots of leafy growth. To keep them productive, trim plants regularly to promote more leaves and prevent them running to flower.

The trouble is, those flowers are full of five-star nectar: in one study, lavender, borage and marjoram were among the top five most popular garden flowers for pollinating insects.

So grow some herbs for you and some for the bees! Sow annuals like basil, coriander and dill every month – then, after harvesting, move to the next batch and leave the first to flower.

THREE MORE WAYS TO SHARE YOUR HARVEST

- Leave brassicas in the ground at the end of the season to burst into nectar-rich flower.

- Leave some windfall apples and plums for birds, wasps and other creatures to enjoy.

- After picking blackcurrants, redcurrants and gooseberries, remove fruit cages and let the birds have the last of the crop.

Lavender,
*Lavandula
angustifolia*

Sharing your harvest with the local wildlife isn't such a hardship when you grow your own. Plant more than you need and you can still enjoy fresh herbs while letting some flower for the bees.

Should I feed the birds?

A GARDEN FULL OF BIRDS is a garden with a healthy ecosystem. But birds can also wreak havoc on your crops, stripping berries and ripping brassicas to shreds. So should you feed the birds – or drive them away?

It's the ultimate gardeners' dilemma. On the one hand, birds offer built-in pest protection; on the other, they can be pests themselves. But you can still have a garden twittering with birds without losing half your harvest: just cover plants when necessary, then let the birds back in.

Putting out extra feed for birds will certainly attract more into your garden, and the more birds there are, the more pests they'll eat. But whether you have five or 500 birds in your garden, you'll need the same protection for your crops.

Cover individual plants, beds or entire areas with bird-proof mesh cages, avoiding plastic netting as it traps wildlife (including birds). For fruit, use 8mm (3/8in) wire mesh;

WATCH THE BIRDIES

Birds leave most crops alone, but some they can't resist.

Brassicas Grow under mesh covers from the start.

Blackcurrants (and most berries) Cover plants or build bespoke fruit cages.

Cherries Fan-trained cherries (below) are easier to protect.

Peas Grow young plants under cages until they're bigger.

Strawberries Cover fruiting rows in galvanized mesh.

close-woven, insect-proof mesh protects non-flowering plants like brassicas. Cover fruit bushes as berries start to colour, removing them once harvesting ends to let the birds back in to clean up any pests.

Q Why are the leaves on my raspberries turning yellow?

YELLOWING LEAVES ARE A CAUSE FOR CONCERN. But when you've had a closer look and ruled out pests, and there's no sign of disease – what else might the problem be?

A Just like people, plants need a balanced diet. This is usually provided by the soil, but some types of soil deliver nutrients better than others. Raspberries, for example, need plenty of iron, but alkaline soils 'lock up' iron, so plants can't access it. One symptom of iron shortage is chlorosis, or yellowing leaves.

When raspberries are deprived of iron, young leaves turn yellow first. If older leaves go yellow (especially tinged red-brown), it's more likely to be magnesium deficiency.

Confirm your diagnosis with a soil test. Simple testing kits tell you your soil's pH: neutral soil has a pH of about seven, above that it's alkaline and soil with a pH less than seven is acidic. Or just look around you: if rhododendrons, camellias and blueberries grow well in your area, you probably have acidic soil. If peonies, clematis and brassicas thrive, it's probably alkaline.

Organic solutions

In alkaline soil, iron is less able to dissolve into a form plants can take up. So plants that need lots of iron to grow well, like raspberries, start suffering. The quick fix is a dose of chelated iron – but this is synthetic,

◀ Yellowing with green leaf veins is a warning sign your plant is going short of nutrients.

so not suitable for organic growers and is only a short-term solution anyway.

You can tolerate low levels of chlorosis as it doesn't usually affect the harvest; a dose of liquid seaweed shores up defences. But you can also improve conditions for your raspberries year on year with regular mulches of naturally acidic materials like composted bracken and bark or well-rotted stable manure, giving them better access to the iron they need.

Raspberry,
Rubus idaeus

MORE MINERAL DEFICIENCIES

Magnesium
Yellowing between leaf veins with red-brown tints may mean your plants are short of magnesium, essential for photosynthesis. Tomatoes, cucumbers and raspberries are susceptible, especially on thin, sandy soils and if you've been overdoing the potassium-rich tomato feed. Cut back on feeding and spray with diluted Epsom salts as a quick organic fix.

Nitrogen
Any plant suffers if it's short of nitrogen, as this is the main growth mineral: look for yellow, sometimes pink-tinged leaves and spindly shoots, especially in spring as winter rains leach nitrogen from the soil. Mulch regularly and you should never go short: in containers and greenhouses, liquid nettle or seaweed feeds put things right.

Calcium
Plants need calcium to make healthy cells. Without it, cells collapse, leaving sunken, blackened patches on tomatoes, aubergines and peppers known as blossom end rot. Most soils have plenty of natural calcium, but thirsty plants can't absorb it properly, so keep the soil consistently damp: automated watering systems can help.

Q My onions are going rotten – what's wrong?

ONIONS ARE MEANT TO FORM FIRM, handsomely rounded bulbs encased in paper-smooth skin. So when you lift your crop in summer to find the bases have turned soft, rotten and white with mould, it's quite a shock. What has happened to your beautiful crop?

A Onion white rot is one of a nasty little gang of soil-borne diseases, all bad news for veg growers. The pathogenic fungus that causes it, *Stromatinia cepivora*, is capable of lurking below ground and reinfecting any new crops for at least 15 years. There's no cure.

Onion,
Allium cepa

▼ Onion white rot is worse in cool, wet summers because the fungus doesn't grow as well when temperatures are above 20°C (68°F).

Most veg gardeners never encounter onion white rot (and a good thing too). It's more common on allotments, as it's easy to spread fungal sclerotia (seed-like structures) in contaminated soil, on tools and muddy boots, or through gifts of spare plants, however well meant.

If you are unlucky enough to suffer an outbreak, there's no point trying to grow onions in that area of the garden again: they'll just be reinfected and your crop ruined. So switch to container growing: most onions grow happily in large pots of peat-free multipurpose compost.

Rotting after storage

If your onions are healthy when you lift them, then turn rotten in storage, don't panic: that's not onion white rot. Another fungal disease, onion neck rot, shows symptoms only after bulbs have been out of the ground for several weeks, in this case bulbs rot from the neck down.

This disease is easier to avoid. Rotate your crop, so you always plant in soil that hasn't had onions growing there for at least three years. Don't give them any extra feed and dry bulbs carefully after lifting your crop, laying them out on racks in a dry, sunny greenhouse or spare room for two weeks. Turn bulbs so they dry evenly, then plait into strings to hang somewhere dry until you need them.

Feeding onions helps encourage sappy, lush growth that is more susceptible to infection.

SOIL-BORNE DISEASES

Most fungi that live in the soil do no harm to plants – some actively help them grow better. But a few are very damaging indeed, and all but impossible to get rid of. Verticillium wilt is caused by a fungal infection of water-carrying xylem cells in tomatoes, aubergines and strawberries, so they can't take up water and wilt. Fusarium wilt is similar and affects asparagus, beans and peas too. Clubroot distorts brassica roots, so they can't absorb nutrients.

Even crop rotation doesn't help, as persistent soil-borne diseases are capable of surviving more than a decade without a target plant. But there is hope for beleaguered veg growers: resistant varieties are now available for all these diseases (though sadly not – yet – for onion white rot). Stick to varieties with a built-in ability to cope and you can keep calm and carry on growing, whatever's lurking in your soil.

Yellowing and wilting of leaves (here on an aubergine leaf) could mean verticillium wilt.

Q Can bugs help protect my plants?

GARDENERS TEND TO THINK OF BUGS AS A NUISANCE – after all, it seems we're forever fending them off our crops so they don't eat our veg before we do. But can bugs help us look after our plants?

Gardening for wildlife isn't always linked to growing vegetables, but it's arguably more important on the veg plot than anywhere else since you're not just helping to boost biodiversity – you're also enlisting the services of your local insect population to help protect your crops.

Wildlife-friendly features should be a part of the scenery. Grow nectar-rich flowers among your veg, install a pond (see page 94), build a bug hotel (see page 172) and leave undisturbed corners and logpiles where bugs can hide, to keep your native biological control system at full throttle.

BIOLOGICAL CONTROLS

For specific problems, you can bring in more bugs as targeted controls against particular pests. Available by mail order, they can be very effective if you follow a few rules.

Know your pest Biological controls are carefully targeted – so identify your pest accurately before ordering.

Time your release It'll be a few weeks before the controls take effect as they need time to multiply. Release them as soon as you see target pests.

Temperature is key Greenhouse controls are from warm climates, so release only once temperatures hit 18–20°C (64–68°F). Outdoor controls such as slug nematodes are active above 5–7°C (40–45°F).

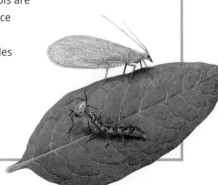

▶ Lacewings are lethal predators of greenfly, blackfly and whitefly.

WHICH BIOCONTROL?

Slugs The nematode *Phasmarhabditis hermaphrodita* (right) infects and kills slugs: sprinkle into the watering can and water on when the soil reaches 5–7°C (40–45°F). Keep the soil damp after applying.

Caterpillars *Steinernema* nematodes destroy caterpillars, rather gruesomely, from the inside out. Add to a spray bottle and spray directly onto caterpillars weekly for three weeks.

Red spider mite Predatory mites *Phytoseiulus* and *Amblyseius* eat red spider mites at all stages of life. They arrive suspended in sawdust to sprinkle onto leaves.

Vine weevil A range of nematodes prey on vine weevil grubs: add to the watering can and apply from midsummer when grubs become active.

Whitefly A parasitoid wasp, *Encarsia formosa*, lays its eggs inside whitefly scales (larvae). These parasitoid wasps arrive attached to a card to hang among your tomato plants.

In healthy ecosystems, populations of 'pest' bugs that want to eat plants are balanced by predators which want to eat them – and often these are other bugs. Maximize nature's pest control by encouraging biodiversity in your garden; you can also add extra bugs – in the form of biological controls – to help tackle specific problems.

Nectar-rich perennial sunflowers are magnets for hoverflies, which will eat your aphids and pollinate your crops too.

Do carrots grow straighter in drainpipes?

DESPERATE TIMES CALL FOR DESPERATE MEASURES. **When your carrots grow wonky every year, no matter what you do, you'd be forgiven for trying more extreme ways to make them straight. What about growing in drainpipes – would that work?**

The roots that eventually develop into carrots start out filigree-fine. As they explore their way downwards, if they hit an obstacle such as a stone, or sometimes just heavy clay, it damages the delicate growth tip – which then forks. Too much rich manure or fertilizer can also burn the growing root, with much the same effect.

The ideal soil for carrots is a light, stone-free, sandy but fertile loam that hasn't been recently manured. If yours falls short, raised beds help; cultivars with shorter roots, known as 'stump-rooted' varieties, also have a better chance of growing straight as they don't need as much depth of soil.

◁ Perfectly straight carrots are the veg gardener's holy grail, and possible even if your garden has less-than-perfect soil.

SHORT CARROTS FOR STONY SOILS

'Paris Market'

'Early Nantes'

'Amsterdam Forcing'

'Burpees Short N Sweet'

'Chantenay Red Cored'

HOW TO GROW CARROTS IN DRAINPIPES

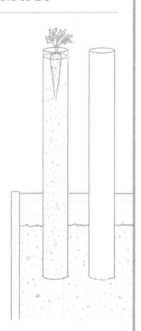

- Stand 60–90cm (2–3ft) lengths of secondhand drainpipe (diameter 10cm/4in) upright in a raised bed frame and bury the bases in soil or sharp sand to a depth of about 15cm (6in).

- Fill with a mix of two parts sieved peat-free potting compost and one part sand, adding a handful of seaweed meal for every 30 litres (7 gallons). Sow three or four seeds of a long-rooted carrot such as 'St Valery' or 'James Scarlet Intermediate' into the top.

- Water from above at first, then once the seedlings are growing strongly start watering from below to encourage roots to head downwards. Once your carrots are ready to harvest, simply pull out of the drainpipe for perfectly straight results, every time.

Crowbar trick

In stony or heavy clay soils, crowbar your way to straight carrots. Drive a crowbar 50–60cm (20–24in) into the ground and wiggle it around to make conical holes about 10cm (4in) apart. Fill with a mix of two parts sieved loam (or leafmould) to one part sand. Water first, then sow a few carrot seeds at each planting station and cover with a little more soil. Pinch out all but the strongest seedling and in a few months' time you should be pulling perfectly straight carrots.

Growing carrots in drainpipes isn't as crazy as it sounds. It's a trick used by generations of exhibition growers to produce long, straight roots which scoop prizes at horticultural shows. But there are other ways to improve your chances of growing straight carrots in the ground, without needing to raid the plumbing supplies!

Is my rhubarb meant to flower?

ON THE WHOLE, RHUBARB IS EASY TO GROW and you'll pull succulent, sweet, pink stalks faster than you can bake them into crumbles. Occasionally, though, the plant sends up flower spikes and everything shudders to a halt. Is that normal?

The most common reason rhubarb plants start flowering is age: clumps older than about five years become overcrowded, producing increasingly skinny, feeble stems as they exhaust the soil's resources.

Cut out the flower stalks for now, but next winter lift and divide the clump. Dig it up and saw into three or four chunks, each with a firm, pale green bud and some roots. Replant your best chunk in rich soil, ideally somewhere else in the garden.

Flowering in rhubarb is a sign of stress, and a warning that your plant isn't happy. So although you can simply cut out the flower spike to keep your plant focused on producing leaves, it's wise to investigate what might be causing the problem.

Climate concern

Climate change is making it more difficult to keep rhubarb plants happy: they can really suffer from being waterlogged in winter or stressed during heatwaves in spring. Give them a cool corner (partial shade is fine) and mulch to lock

◀ Cut out rhubarb flowers as soon as possible and well before they set seed, or your harvest may suffer.

moisture in and to open up the soil, so surplus rain can drain away.

Some varieties are more sensitive and prone to bolting than others, especially older cultivars like 'Victoria'. It's also important to leave newly planted rhubarb to establish without picking for a year or two. Also aim to stop pulling stalks altogether by midsummer to allow the plant to build up reserves for another superb performance next season.

Beating the bolt

Lots of plants start flowering earlier than normal – or bolting – when they're stressed. It's a natural response to danger: the plant is reproducing as quickly as possible in case the threat turns out to be fatal. As it flowers, it diverts its energies away from leaf production – so your harvest ends.

Many leafy veg, including lettuce, rocket, coriander and spinach, prefer cool, damp conditions and bolt as soon as they dry out or get too hot. Concentrate water supplies on these crops to keep them productive and give them a shady spot; planting under taller plants or in shade tunnels helps.

Often it's easier simply to take a break from growing these heat-sensitive crops through high summer: start sowing again once the weather cools and they'll stay leafier for longer – often well into winter.

BOLTING BENEFITS

If veg plants bolt, turn it into an opportunity. Rocket (above) and radish flowers are delicious to eat, and coriander seed is a valuable spice for crushing into curries. You can't eat rhubarb flowers, but you can arrange them in vases as unusual floral arrangements.

Coriander, *Coriandrum sativum*

Chapter 5

Harvest and Beyond

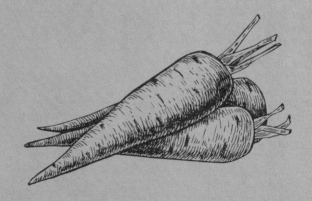

Can you ever guarantee a good harvest?

GROWING YOUR OWN FOOD CAN SEEM LIKE A LOTTERY.
One year everything falls into place; then the next, nothing goes
right and you're about ready to hang up your trowel. Can you
ever guarantee a predictable harvest?

At the start of each year, plan an outline for your veg-growing season. It will almost certainly change, but it gives you a framework for a steady supply of food throughout the year, as well as making sure you have enough of the food you like to eat and in the right quantities.

There are simple online garden planners available, or you can just sketch out your veg plot to scale and fill in the beds with what you're planning to grow. Mark in the sowing and harvesting dates for each crop, so you know when beds will empty, and then you can plan what to refill them with too.

No season is the same, and you'll have at least one crop failure most years. But don't blame yourself: weather conditions that suit one crop can be a major setback for another. So grow a wide variety of veg, plan carefully, but be flexible, and you can still count on a decent harvest – whatever the season throws at you.

Built-in weatherproofing

As you're developing your masterplan, build in some insurance against the inevitable twists and turns of the veg-growing year. These strategies buffer your plot against the vicissitudes of the weather – increasingly important as the climate changes. While you may not harvest what or when you'd planned, you will still have plenty to enjoy.

◀ Sow broad beans in autumn for an
early crop the following summer – then
sow again in early spring in case your
first batch comes a cropper.

RESILIENCE STRATEGIES

Grow a wide range of crops
Peas like damp, cool summers but will fail in heatwaves; French beans bask in sunshine. So sow both – then whatever happens at least one will succeed.

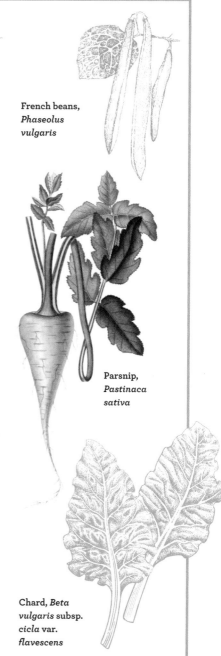

French beans,
Phaseolus vulgaris

Look for super-reliable varieties
Early-maturing tomatoes like 'Ailsa Craig' do well in both good and bad summers; self-pollinating runner beans like 'Moonlight' produce pods whether it's sunny or not.

Grow crops that are less weather-sensitive
Chard, kale, broad beans, parsnips, leeks and slow-to-bolt, loose-leaved lettuces give you a harvest more or less whatever the weather.

Parsnip,
Pastinaca sativa

Make insurance sowings
Don't just sow once: sow two or three batches, one a month early, one at the usual time and one a month late, so at least one is likely to catch an ideal window of weather.

Be ready for anything
Have cloches to hand for popping over salads and seedlings if late frost strikes, or to keep excess water off in endless rainy spells so they don't get waterlogged.

Chard, *Beta vulgaris* subsp. *cicla* var. *flavescens*

How do I know my winter squash is ripe?

YOU'VE BEEN WATCHING THE FRUITS SWELL ALL SUMMER, and now they're deepening to a rich burned orange – but does that mean your winter squash are ripe? How can you tell?

Colour is a good indicator, but sometimes squash aren't orange but pale yellow, grey or even green when they're ripe, so it can be hard to tell. Help fruits ripen by exposing them to the sun and leave on the plant as long as possible before cutting.

Sometimes it's obvious when your crops are ready: you wouldn't pick a tomato while it was still green, for example. But occasionally a little more judgement is needed.

As squash fruits start to colour, lift them onto bricks to let air circulate underneath and help the skins harden.

IS IT READY YET? A FEW TIPS...

• Pick over your plot every few days to catch your veg at the peak of perfection.

• Hold pea pods up against the light before picking, so you can see if the peas inside are fully developed.

• Chillies get hotter as they ripen. For milder chillies, pick them green, but for the full mouth-numbing experience, wait until they colour up.

Remove any leaves directly shading the fruit and turn the fruit carefully from time to time, while still attached to the plant, so all sides are exposed to the sun.

When the plant has died back (or before the first frost) and the skin of your squash is hard and sounds hollow when knocked, you can be sure it's ripe and ready to harvest.

Should I wash the mud off my potatoes before storing?

MAINCROP POTATOES KEEP FOR AGES AFTER HARVESTING.
But when you dig up your crop inevitably it comes up covered in
mud – do you have to wash it off before storing?

Choose a dry day for harvesting, and carefully dig up the entire crop at once. Spread the potatoes out on the soil to dry for a couple of hours, turning once or twice to make sure the skins dry off evenly; then pick them over, choosing only perfect specimens to store (eat the rest straightaway). Gently brush off excess dirt, then tip your crop into hessian or paper sacks.

If you have grown your potatoes the no-dig way – burying them in mulch, then earthing up with more compost as they grow – they come out almost clean with very little mud at all.

A little dirt on your spuds both protects the skins and helps them store better.

Washing your potatoes removes the layer of natural protection they get from a little dirt. You may also damage skins by scrubbing, and washing makes them too damp, so they rot in storage. It's better to 'cure' (dry) the skins to help preserve your spuds in mint condition.

Storing your crop

Choose somewhere dry, dark and cool (5–10°C/40–50°F) to store your spuds. Sheds are usually too damp, but garages or unheated spare rooms often work well. Keep potatoes completely dark – double-bag them or put them in a cupboard. And check stores regularly, removing any that are deteriorating. If you have trouble with mice raiding your potato stash, then hang sacks from sturdy hooks where even the most athletic thief is unlikely to reach them.

Q Help! I can't eat all this!

THERE COMES A DAY, USUALLY IN EARLY AUTUMN, when you open the gate to the veg plot and realize absolutely everything needs picking, right now. You fill buckets and still there's more – so what can you do with it all?

A void gluts where you can by sowing fast-growing salads, spinach, beetroot and annual herbs little and often to harvest steadily throughout the year. That's not possible, though, for crops that take all season to mature, then produce their crop in one big flood: so your only option is to get cooking!

Dealing with your surplus

Processing and storing your surplus crops means you can keep them for eating later, and don't have to waste all that lovely food you've grown.

Fully ripe marrows, winter squash and pumpkins store for months on racks somewhere cool and dry. Wrap

Plum, *Prunus domestica*

cooking apples in newspaper to lay in crates, and pack root veg in damp sand (see page 201).

Summer veg such as peas and beans freeze well as they are; grow twice as much as you need to create a deliberate surplus that you can stash in the freezer for winter. Rhubarb, tomatoes and apples need to be chopped and cooked before freezing. You can also bottle fruit and tomatoes (see page 206).

Vegetables with a high water content, like courgettes, don't freeze easily. So make them into pasta sauces,

A

Glut crops such as tomatoes, courgettes, runner beans, apples and plums are generous to the point of being overwhelming. But gluts are also your opportunity to squirrel away your summer surplus: it may feel like a lot of work now, but in midwinter, you'll be glad you did.

GLUT-BUSTING CHUTNEY RECIPE

This chutney recipe turns any fruit or veg you have too much of into a fragrant, spicy relish.

△ Courgettes make wonderful chutney – it's a great way to use up fruits that have grown a little too large.

You will need
- 3kg (7lb) glut vegetables or fruit (cooking apples, courgettes, tomatoes, squash), diced
- 500g (1lb 2oz) onions, diced
- 500g (1lb 2oz) sultanas
- 500g (1lb 2oz) soft brown sugar
- 1 litre (2 pints) malt vinegar
- 2 tsp dried chilli
- 1 tsp salt
- 5cm (2in) piece of fresh ginger root, chopped
- 12 cloves
- 12 black peppercorns
- 1 tsp coriander seeds

1 Put the vegetables and fruit and in a heavy-based pan with the sultanas, sugar, vinegar, chilli and salt. Bundle the spices up in knotted muslin and add to the pan.

2 Simmer the chutney slowly, uncovered, for 4–6 hours, stirring occasionally. It's ready when you can draw a wooden spoon through and leave a channel.

3 Ladle into sterilized jars (see page 207), seal with a waxed paper disc, screw lids on and leave for 2–3 months to mature.

pies and soups first for home-grown frozen ready meals.

Sugar, salt and vinegar are natural preservatives and keep for months; you can also salt or ferment your surplus (see page 207).

Once you've stored all the surplus that you can, start spreading the love. Swap with friends or sign up to food sharing apps (see page 211) so nothing goes to waste.

Can I keep beetroot in the ground all winter?

ROOT VEG, SUCH AS BEETROOT, HAVE BUILT-IN RESERVES which means that even after they've stopped growing at the end of the season, they still stay in good condition in the ground until you're ready to eat them. But how long can you leave them there?

Roots eaten young and tender, such as beetroot, carrots and turnips, carry on growing slowly during milder weather – so by the end of winter they're often big and over-mature, with woody, inedible cores and little flavour. You'll also find that as autumn wears on and other food sources become scarce, slugs are all too happy to chew on your root veg, leaving you with little that's worth harvesting.

Celeriac, *Apium graveolens* var. *rapaceum*

Beetroot, *Beta vulgaris*

Harvest early

It's much better to lift beetroot by the autumn when no larger than a tennis ball. While you're at it, lift carrots, celeriac and winter radish too. Parsnips and swede stay good in the ground for longer, but are still less woody if harvested early. It's true they taste sweeter after frost, but in more southerly areas frosts are becoming increasingly scarce anyway: keeping them in the fridge should produce a similar effect.

HOW TO STORE ROOT VEG THROUGH WINTER

- Dampen some sand or sawdust with water.

- Use this to cover the base of your crate to a depth of 5–8cm (2–3in).

- Lay your roots on top, side by side but not touching.

- Cover with another 5–8cm (2–3in) of sand.

- Repeat until the last layer of stored veg is covered, ending with a layer of sand.

- Place somewhere dry and very cool – ideally 5–8°C (40–50°F).

Leave to dry for an hour or two in the sun, then brush off the worst of the dirt. Twist off the tops, then pack the lot into crates for storing.

Fending off thieves

Stored roots are utterly irresistible to mice and rats: once they get a sniff of your stash they'll break into the most heavily fortified shed to find it. So a rodent-proof storage area is essential.

Build a mouse-proof cage by stapling 6mm (¼in)-gauge wire mesh (available from DIY stores and larger pet shops) securely over a wooden box frame. You can also use secondhand galvanized metal dustbins and animal feed bins – though they must be well ventilated or your stores will rot. Close storage units tightly, with doors bolted and lids weighed down with bricks, and your root veg should stay safe for months.

Most roots – including beetroot, carrots and parsnips – are biennial: they build up reserves in big fat roots in the first year, then flower in their second. So they're designed to stay in the ground all winter: the trouble is, they steadily lose eating quality over time. Lift and store them early to enjoy them at their best.

A mouse can squeeze through a hole just 6mm (¼in) wide, so keep your stores well protected.

Can I make my own fruit juice?

FRESHLY SQUEEZED FRUIT JUICE is full of natural sugars and vitamins, and a great energy-boosting way to start your day. Orange juice is beyond those of us who live in cooler climates, but can you turn other home-grown fruits into juice?

🔺 Carrots make a colourful vitamin-rich drink: chop roughly, pulp in a blender, then strain (try mixing 50:50 with home-made apple juice).

Home-grown juices take breakfast to another level. They're vibrant with flavour, additive-free and contain mostly natural sugars, too. Berry juices are easy to make; although apple and pear juice requires specialist equipment, club together with friends and it's a wonderful way to put surplus fruit to good use.

Crush almost any fruit and you'll extract copious amounts of juice. It's so full of natural fructose there's hardly any need to add more sugar: all you have to do is bottle it.

You can make juice from berries (including grapes) without any special equipment. Pick over and clean your berries and load them into a pan with just enough water to make them float. Heat to a simmer, then mash roughly and simmer for another 10 minutes. Stir in sugar, if needed, then leave to cool. Finally, pour through a sieve lined with muslin and then dilute 50:50 with water to drink.

Apple juicing

Apple and pear juicing is an autumn tradition: get together with tree-owning friends to rent or buy juicing equipment or find a juicing event near you where they supply the gear and you supply the fruit.

Collect all fruit, including windfalls, then wash, remove stalks, leaves and bruised bits, and chop roughly (no need to peel or core). Next feed through a scratter to crush the fruit into a gloopy mush, known as pomace. You can also put the fruit in a bucket

FRUIT CORDIAL

You will need

- 400g (14oz) blackcurrants, raspberries or redcurrants
- 250g (9oz) caster sugar (vary to taste)
- 250ml (^{1}/2 pint) water
- Juice of a lemon

Blackcurrants,
Ribes nigrum

1 De-stalk and gently wash the fruit, then place in a large saucepan with the sugar and water and heat gently, stirring until the sugar dissolves. Simmer for five minutes, then add the lemon juice.

2 Return to a slow simmer and cook for another five minutes, then leave to cool.

3 Strain through a sieve lined with muslin, then decant into sterilized bottles (see page 207). Dilute like squash for drinking. Cordial keeps for a month in the fridge or you can freeze some for later too.

Redcurrants, *Ribes rubrum*

and whack it with a wooden post (food processors make too good a job of it). Tip your mush into the press, lined with a straining bag. Fold over the top of the bag, then screw down the press to extract the cloudy, brown, delicious juice. Drink your freshly made juice within two to three days and pour the rest into plastic bottles to freeze immediately.

Can I use seeds from my vegetables to grow next year?

COMMERCIAL VEG SEED PRODUCTION is a multinational business. The seeds in your (often plastic-coated) packet have likely flown miles to get to you: most are treated with pesticides, too. So can you avoid the environmental price tag by saving seeds from your own veg?

SEED-SAVING TECHNIQUES

Tomatoes

• Scoop out pulp and seed from a very ripe tomato with a teaspoon.

• Spread over kitchen towel and leave to dry for two weeks.

• Store kitchen towel (with seeds attached) in a paper envelope.

• To sow, lay the towel on a tray of seed compost, cover with more compost and water for a forest of seedlings.

Beans

• Wait until pods have turned yellow at the end of the season.

• Shuck out the beans onto a tray to finish drying indoors for two weeks.

Peas

• Leave pods on the plant until they're papery brown.

• Pop open the pods and collect your ready-dried seeds.

Lettuces

• Once the flowerheads turn straw-coloured and most seeds are ripe, cut off the whole head.

• In a bucket, gently rub off as much seed as comes away easily.

• Shake in a kitchen sieve until the fluffy chaff rises to the top and you can pick it off.

Saving your own seed is a more sustainable way to garden and since every home-saved seed is from parents that grew well for you, you know they're pre-programmed to succeed in your particular microclimate. Home-saved seed is also super fresh and keeps for ages; plus it's completely free.

Always save seed from your best plants: mark prize performers with a piece of red wool, so you'll remember not to pick and eat your would-be seeds! Vigorous growers and heavy croppers, plus naturally disease-resistant plants, will pass on their good genes to their offspring.

Start by saving seed from the four reliably self-fertile veg: tomatoes, beans, peas and lettuces, then graduate to cross-pollinating veg like brassicas and chillies. A simple way to avoid unwanted cross-pollination is to grow only one variety (or let just one variety flower), as then you'll be certain you'll get back the same variety as the parent. This applies to self-fertile veg too, as they can still be pollinated by insects.

PROMISCUOUS PUMPKINS

Cucurbits – that's pumpkins, squash, courgettes, melons and cucumbers – cross-pollinate very easily, so you'll have to hand-pollinate fruit to get the same variety again.

When female flower buds (with a miniature fruit behind) start to colour, tie them shut with wool. Get a straight-stemmed male flower, remove the petals, then untie the female flower and dab the male anthers into the centre. Tie the bud shut again: once the fruit is mature you can safely save its seed.

Winter squash, *Cucurbita maxima* **'Red Kuri'**

Should I freeze, bottle, dry or ferment?

AFTER A LONG AND SUCCESSFUL SEASON you won't want to waste an ounce of your hard-won harvest. But when faced with a mountain of veg to process, how do you choose the best technique to preserve it all?

◀ Make your own Maraschino cherries for cocktails and desserts by bottling fresh cherries in syrup.

Freezing is still the number one choice for preserving most types of fruit and vegetables. But freezers require power and the freezing process can break down some vitamins as well as affect flavour and texture (though peas, broad beans and most berries freeze with hardly any loss of quality).

Other, older ways of preserving produce require more processing, but let you store your surplus in ordinary kitchen cupboards. It's also fun and deeply satisfying.

Bottling (canning)

Suitable for tomatoes and most fruit.

Bottle most fruit whole, but cut peaches in half to remove stones, and peel, core and quarter apples and pears. Pack tightly into preserving jars, then cover with syrup (225g/8oz sugar to 600ml/1 pint water). Close the lids and stand in a pan of water up to the necks. Bring to a simmer very slowly, over one and a half hours. Check the temperature with a thermometer: most fruits must stay at 82°C (180°F) for 30 minutes.

For tomatoes, peel and then toss in lemon juice and salt. Pack into jars and proceed as above, but slightly warmer (88°C/190°F for 40 minutes). Lift jars out and allow to cool.

Drying

Suitable for tomatoes, apples, thin-skinned chillies and berries (as leathers).

String chillies together with a needle and thread and hang somewhere sunny to dry. Slice apples and cut tomatoes in half, then bake on your oven's lowest setting for 8–12 hours.

Fruit leathers are great candy substitutes for kids: cook fruit into a purée with honey and lemon juice, line baking trays with greaseproof paper, then pour in your liquidized fruit. Cook in the oven at 100°C (212°F) for six to eight hours; once cool, cut into strips.

HOW TO STERILIZE JARS AND BOTTLES

Jam jars, bottles and fermenting jars must be scrupulously clean. Wash thoroughly or put them through the dishwasher, then heat in the oven at 100°C (212°F) for 15 minutes to sterilize.

Fermenting

Suitable for white cabbage, carrots and cucumbers.

Chop your veg and sprinkle with coarse sea salt. Massage in thoroughly, then pack tightly into a sterilized wide-mouthed jar with spices. Push a clean plastic bag filled with water into the top to stop air getting in and leave to ferment (the veg will 'burp' as gases escape). Top up with water to keep the veg covered and start tasting after five days; once the veg has a pleasant tangy-but-sour flavour, it's ready.

Many traditional preserving methods became redundant when fridges and freezers arrived. But now many cooks are rediscovering salting, drying and bottling, not least for their health benefits. They're also a great fallback when your freezer is full.

▶ Wash everything, from bowls to jars to your hands, so they're scrupulously clean before you start fermenting to avoid accidentally contaminating the mix.

To blanch or not to blanch?

BLANCHING IS OFTEN RECOMMENDED just before freezing: the idea is you drop just-harvested veg into fast-boiling water for a few minutes before packing them into the freezer. But is it really necessary?

The veg-growing world is split when it comes to blanching. Some people say it's a must for keeping your veg in good condition in the freezer. Others just bypass the whole process, saying they don't notice any difference in quality. So experiment, taste the results and then draw your own conclusions on this!

HOW TO BLANCH VEGETABLES

You will need
- Large pan
- Strainer, blanching basket or mesh bag
- Timer
- Bowl of iced water

▼ Break cauliflower heads into florets, then blanch for three minutes before freezing.

1 Wash and prepare your veg, trimming off stalks and shucking beans from pods.

2 Fill the pan with plenty of water and bring to a fast boil.

3 Fill the strainer, basket or bag with veg and lower into the water.

4 Start your timer the moment the water returns to a boil.

5 Once the time is up, transfer the blanched veg into cold water straightaway to stop it cooking.

6 Leave the veg in cold water for the same time as for blanching, stirring occasionally.

7 Drain and pack into freezer containers or bags.

◀ Broad beans are best frozen young; if the scar where the bean met the pod has darkened to black, make broad bean hummus instead.

A Heating fresh vegetables briefly but fiercely kills off enzymes that cause deterioration in storage. But it's important to do it right, otherwise you end up inadvertently pre-cooking your veg. And if you're planning to eat your frozen veg fairly soon, you can manage without blanching, saving time, effort and energy.

Freezing without blanching

Many veg are just as good frozen without blanching. Podding peas and beans (especially broad beans) come out just as good whether you blanch or not, while tomatoes, onions and peppers lose their texture on cooking anyway, so it doesn't matter either way.

Give your veg a quick wash and shake them dry. Spread veg in a single layer on a baking tray, then freeze overnight. Next day, pack into bags or containers: they'll then stay individually frozen so you can grab a handful without having to defrost a whole block. Peas, broad beans and French beans are best frozen just as they are: don't even bother to top and tail French beans as you can do that just before cooking, while still frozen, and they'll keep their texture better.

Vegetables that haven't been blanched are just as safe and tasty to eat. They do start losing quality if you leave them in the freezer too long, though, so eat unblanched vegetables within three to six months.

BLANCHING TIMES

2 minutes Sliced carrots, peas and sweet peppers cut into strips.

3 minutes Beans, broccoli and cauliflower.

4 minutes Brussels sprouts and sweetcorn kernels (cool for twice this time).

7 minutes Whole sweetcorn cobs (cool for twice this time).

Will one bad apple really ruin the whole barrel?

LATE-MATURING APPLES, including Cox, Russets and most cooking apples, keep for months after harvest. But what if they've picked up a touch of scab or a few have been nibbled? Does it matter if the apples you store are less than perfect?

As you harvest your apples, inspect each one and set aside any with blemishes, however small, to eat or cook straightaway.

It's very easy to miss damage, especially light bruising (one reason to handle apples carefully). So wrap each apple individually in newspaper: this stops it touching its neighbours in store and slows the spread of infection.

Inspect your stores every few weeks, unpacking and repacking everything to check it's all still sound. Take any apples that are bad out promptly and the rest should stay in perfect condition.

As soon as apples, or any other fruit or vegetable, are damaged they begin to deteriorate. If they're in store the rot spreads quickly to other healthy produce, ruining the lot. So only store perfect specimens.

The science of storing

Bad patches on apples are sometimes caused by bacteria, fungi or insects which go into storage with the apple and happily visit and infect nearby apples too.

However, rotting in storage is also caused by the hormone ethylene. This is produced as fruits ripen, but also in response to stresses such as bruises or wounds. So damaged fruits give off more ethylene than normal, triggering their neighbours to ripen faster until they become overripe and rot.

▽ Apples stay good to eat for three or four months, as long as they are undamaged and prepared well for storage.

Is getting tips from social media a good idea?

SOCIAL MEDIA PLATFORMS are awash with gardening advice on everything from how to sow seeds to the finer points of grafting tomatoes. But how much of it can you rely on to help you garden better?

Start by following trusted organizations such as the Royal Horticultural Society, Garden Organic and the Royal Botanic Gardens, Kew. Your algorithm will then suggest gardening-related accounts for you, but check the profile before following.

Fill your feed with head gardeners, professional growers and leading garden writers to tap into a rich seam of advice backed by experience.

Listening to podcasts often introduces you to up-and-coming new gardeners and influencers who may not have a high profile in conventional media. If they've got a strong, engaged following and a YouTube channel or IGTV (Instagram TV) feed, you'll often find they're the ones pioneering ground-breaking ideas, which can change the way you garden forever.

WHICH PLATFORM FOR WHAT?

Facebook for gardening groups where you can ask advice.

Instagram for inspirational pictures and IGTV to watch how the experts do it.

Twitter to debate the hottest topics and glean bite-size tips from true professionals.

Pinterest for links to DIY projects and how-tos.

TikTok for snappy how-to videos and quirky snippets of plant-related inspiration.

These days the best gardeners in the world are at your fingertips, sharing decades of experience via bite-size chunks of wisdom. Social media is where all the interesting ideas are in gardening; to find them, follow trusted accounts, stay sceptical and back up claims with your own research.

How do I plait my garlic?

AFTER LIFTING YOUR SUN-RIPENED GARLIC and onions at the end of summer, it's traditional (and looks gorgeous) to store them hung up, in long plaits. But how do you plait garlic?

HOW TO PLAIT GARLIC

Dry your crop thoroughly for a fortnight, then select your best bulbs for storing, removing any that are damaged or small for eating right away. Then brush off any dirt and trim away the roots.

1 Take three bulbs and lay on the table with leaves towards you.

2 Weave the leaves over each other to start your plait, pulling the bulbs in tightly.

3 Holding the three leaf bundles apart, add another bulb to the bunch, pulling it in tight so it's snug against its neighbours: add its leaves to the central bundle.

4 Pull the right-hand bundle across, then add another bulb, pulling that in snug too.

5 Add the new bulb's leaves to the central bundle.

6 Repeat until you have a plait about 60cm (2ft) long.

7 Plait the rest of the foliage to the bottom and finish off with a knot.

Garlic is easy to plait together using the long, strong leaves; simply feed in more garlic heads as you work down the plait. Onions are trickier as they have shorter, weaker top growth, so you'll need to weave them through a loop of string to hold them in place.

◀ Whenever you need a bulb of garlic, just twist or cut one from your plait: the rest can stay there until next time.

Plaiting garlic and onion helps your crop keep longer as it lets plenty of air reach the bulbs. It's also a really convenient way to keep your crop within easy reach of the kitchen.

Kitchens themselves aren't the best place to hang your garlic and onion strings, as they tend to be too warm and humid. So keep only the plait you're actually using in the kitchen: hang the rest in a cool, dry spare room or garage where they'll keep better.

▶ Trim off the roots before you plait, and rub off very loose skin (don't overdo this as the skin helps to protect the bulb).

Plaiting onions

Onions have weaker stems, so they're plaited slightly differently. Prepare your crop as for garlic, but trim the top growth to 10–15cm (4–6in). Then make a 60cm (2ft) loop of strong string and hang on a hook.

Make a small loop in the bottom of the string and poke the stem of an onion through. Pull it tight – the weight of the onion holds it in place. Take your next onion, pull it in close to the string, then weave the stem in and out of the string underneath the bulb itself – when you slide the onion down it should sit on top of its own stem, holding it firmly in place.

Repeat this for each bulb, turning the plait slightly as you work, so the onions are evenly spaced around the plait. Stop once the plait is getting heavy and hang up to store.

How can I make my harvest last longer?

HARVESTING IS THE HIGH POINT OF THE GARDENING YEAR, **when all your hard work is rewarded with armfuls of mouth-wateringly good food. You want it to go on forever – so how do you make sure you're picking for as long as possible?**

The better your plants are feeling, the more they produce. If they're stressed and start bolting (see page 191), go thirsty or fall prey to pests, your harvest crashes. So keep them growing strongly: concentrate water supplies on plants in full production and stamp out problems promptly.

Some plants naturally produce crops longer than others. You'll pick cut-and-come-again lettuces for weeks, while heading lettuces are over in a single cut; runner beans produce a steady stream of pods from midsummer until the first frosts.

Runner beans,
Phaseolus coccineus

Keep your veg in tip-top condition and sow repeatedly throughout the season. Major on varieties that naturally crop for ages. Manage your harvest: pick little and often, don't be too quick to clear crops, and add extra shelter to keep the party going.

Max out your harvest

Try to pick your veg at daybreak, as that's when the sun hasn't yet had time to evaporate away any moisture. For tomatoes, strawberries and melons, though, hold fire until the sun has warmed their skins, to develop their aromatic, rich flavour to the full.

You can keep picking beyond the initial harvest by using little tricks to persuade plants to produce for longer.

Courgettes and beans think they're done for the year if you let seeds develop. Pick every few days to catch the crop young, so they keep producing.

As long as you don't remove the central growing tip, leafy veg – including lettuces, kale and mizuna – will produce more leaves to replace any they lose. The plants develop a stem, so look a bit odd, but you'll extend your harvest by weeks.

Cabbages and calabrese often resprout if you leave them in the ground, so don't be too quick to dig up the stumps and clear your crop.

Salads stay pickable much longer if you pop a glass cloche over the row as the weather turns colder in autumn.

Chive, *Allium schoenoprasum*

HARVEST YOUR EXTRAS

Don't stop after you've picked the obvious bits: there are so many more harvests to gather!

Beetroot leaves
Pick young to eat raw in salads, leaving enough behind to keep the plant healthy.

Broad bean shoots
Snip out the top 10cm (4in) once plants are mature and wilt in butter.

Brussels sprout tops
Cut away the cabbagey head in late autumn.

Pea shoots
The curly tendrils are sweet and crunchy: pinch off shoots just above a pair of leaves.

Squash shoots
Cutting back tips keeps plants in bounds – and they're delicious sautéed with garlic.

Pea (*Pisum sativum***) shoot**

What's square foot gardening?

WHEN SPACE IS LIMITED or you just need to cram a lot of different crops into a small area, clever techniques like square foot gardening can really help. But what is square foot gardening – and how does it work?

SAMPLE SQUARE FOOT PLAN

Courgette 'Patio Star' (1 plant)	Lettuce 'Salad Bowl' (4 plants)	French bean 'Cobra' (2 plants)	French bean 'Cobra' (2 plants)
Beetroot 'Boltardy' (9 plants)	Leek 'King Richard' (9 plants)	French bean 'Cobra' (2 plants)	French bean 'Cobra' (2 plants)
Carrot 'Paris Market Atlas' (16 plants)	Calabrese 'Matsuri' (1 plant)	Salad rocket (broad-cast-sown)	Chard 'Swiss' (1 plant)
Bush tomato 'Losetto' (1 plant)	Turnip 'Tokyo Cross' (12 plants)	Baby-leaf kale 'Red Russian' (broad-cast-sown)	Nasturtium 'Empress of India' (1 plant)

You can adapt existing raised beds or build yourself a new square-foot bed from scratch out of old scaffold boards. This is intensive growing, so conditions should be as good as you can make them: a sunny, sheltered spot on rich soil is ideal.

Fill new raised beds with a 50:50 mix of garden compost and topsoil, and mulch existing beds. Then divide up the space. Sink hazel sticks into the ground and tie strings across. You can also drive screws halfway into the top edges of the bed at intervals and tie string to those.

Size doesn't matter

A square foot is the minimum size for each patch, so don't make squares any smaller or the plants won't have enough room. You can, however, make them larger or rectangular: as long as the space is divided up roughly equally.

Sow a different crop into each square. Plants suitable for square foot growing include upright growers like leeks and fast-growing salad crops. Stick to patio varieties for larger plants like courgettes, and give them a corner square so they won't swamp their neighbours. Reserve four squares for climbing beans, so you can train them up a wigwam, with one upright in

Square foot gardening divides any space up into smaller patches, each planted with a different type of crop. At its most intensive, it lets you grow as many as nine different types of vegetables in a bed just 1m (3ft) square, giving you a really impressive variety to pick from even the tiniest veg plots.

each square, and plant leafy crops like lettuce or spinach alongside as they prefer the shade cast by taller plants.

The number of plants in each square depends on their eventual size. So you'd plant just one courgette, but nine beetroots or four lettuces. Broadcast-sow crops grown close together, like baby-leaf salads, simply scattering seed across the square.

▼ Use square foot techniques to create salad or herb gardens crammed with interesting flavours and textures.

◀ Square foot gardens stay productive right through the year if you replace or resow each square as soon as it's cleared, with the same or a new crop to harvest in the next season.

Further reading

Once you venture into the brave new world of sustainable food growing, you begin a journey that will change everything you ever thought you knew about gardening. Many of these new ideas I've only been able to touch on in this book – so explore further with those pioneering new ways of thinking about how we grow our food.

Back Garden Seed Saving
Sue Stickland
Eco-Logic Books, 2008

Charles Dowding's No Dig Gardening: From Weeds to Vegetables Easily and Quickly
Charles Dowding
No Dig Garden, 2020

RHS Grow for Flavour
James Wong
Mitchell Beazley, 2015

Growing Self-Sufficiency
Sally Nex
Green Books, 2017

Grow Your Own Fruit (4th edition)
Ken Muir
Ken Muir, 2007

RHS Grow Your Own Crops in Pots
Kay Maguire
Mitchell Beazley, 2022

RHS Grow Your Own Veg and Fruit Bible
Carol Klein
Mitchell Beazley, 2020

Grow Your Own Vegetables
Joy Larkcom
Frances Lincoln 2002

RHS How Can I Help Hedgehogs?
Helen Bostock and Sophie Collins
Mitchell Beazley, 2019

RHS How to Grow Plants from Seeds
Sophie Collins
Mitchell Beazley, 2021

How to Grow Perennial Vegetables
Martin Crawford
Green Books, 2012

How to Grow the Low Carbon Way
Sally Nex
Dorling Kindersley, 2021

How to Make Your Own Drinks
Susy Atkins
Mitchell Beazley, 2011

Managing Water Sustainably in the Garden and Landscape
Nigel Dunnett & Andy Clayden
Timber Press, 2007

Pam the Jam: The Book of Preserves
Pam Corbin
Bloomsbury Publishing, 2019

RHS Seeds
Jekka McVicar
Kyle Cathie, 2012

Small Green Roofs
Nigel Dunnett, Dusty Gedge & John Little
Timber Press, 2011

The Climate Change Garden
Sally Morgan & Kim Stoddart
Green Rocket, 2019

The Garden Jungle
Prof. Dave Goulson
Vintage, 2020

*The Vegetable Gardener's Guide
to Permaculture: Creating an
Edible Ecosystem*
Christopher Shein & Julie Thompson
Timber Press, 2013

Wilding
Isabella Tree
Picador, 2019

Web resources

Charles Dowding's No Dig Gardening
charlesdowding.co.uk

Garden Organic
gardenorganic.org.uk

Living Roofs
livingroofs.org

Olio (food sharing website)
olioex.com

Royal Horticultural Society
rhs.org.uk

About the author

Sally Nex is a professional gardener and award-winning garden writer, and grows most of her vegetables, fruit and herbs herself in a wild and woolly hillside garden in rural Somerset, southwest England. For the last ten years she has been pioneering more environmentally friendly approaches to vegetable growing, campaigning against the use of plastic in gardens and encouraging more self-reliant, low-carbon methods of growing.

Index

Credits